WHY I LEFT, WHY I STAYED

*Conversations on Christianity
Between an Evangelical Father
and His Humanist Son*

TONY CAMPOLO
and BART CAMPOLO

HarperOne
An Imprint of HarperCollinsPublishers

HarperOne

WHY I LEFT, WHY I STAYED. Copyright © 2017 by Anthony Campolo and Bart Campolo. All rights reserved. Printed in the United States of America. No part of this book may be used or reproduced in any manner whatsoever without written permission except in the case of brief quotations embodied in critical articles and reviews. For information, address HarperCollins Publishers, 195 Broadway, New York, NY 10007.

HarperCollins books may be purchased for educational, business, or sales promotional use. For information, please email the Special Markets Department at SPsales@harpercollins.com.

FIRST HARPERCOLLINS PAPERBACK EDITION PUBLISHED IN 2018

Designed by Paul Barrett

Library of Congress Cataloging-in-Publication Data is available upon request.

ISBN 978–0–06–241538–7

18 19 20 21 22   LSC(H)   10 9 8 7 6 5 4 3 2 1

To good friends and families everywhere, ceaselessly striving to love one another across the great divide of faith. We are proud to be among you.

CONTENTS

PREFACE

WE ARE NOT UNUSUAL. Many Christian parents are struggling, both emotionally and spiritually, because their children have left the Christian faith. For some, the result is tension, acrimony, and alienation. Reasonable and caring conversations in such families often become impossible.

Our family has struggled as well, but we haven't stopped talking—or caring. Hopefully, this book models a graceful way to process what has become an increasingly common crisis, while also serving as a safe forum for those struggling with doubts and questions about the Christian faith. Such issues can sometimes feel too overwhelming and threatening to discuss openly with friends and relatives, but we think a dialogue like ours can make room for our readers to think through and meditate on some of life's ultimate issues.

In this book, we want you to see how conversations about heartrending differences can be carried out in such a way that it can truly be said that both a Christian father and his human-ist son heeded the plea of the apostle Paul to be kind, tender-hearted, and forgiving to one another in all things.

Tony Campolo
Bryn Mawr, Pennsylvania

Bart Campolo
Los Angeles, California

FOREWORD

by Peggy Campolo

I AM HONORED THAT MY husband and our son asked me to contribute to this book, but I wish there was no need for it. The story of how Bart came to lose his faith and how this change affected both his life and his father's contains much pain and many misunderstandings. I have lived in the midst of that pain and misunderstanding, loving both men with all my heart and finding much to admire in each of them.

I never could have predicted this turn of events. When Bart was a little boy, he was such a kind, considerate, and caring child that I often wondered if he was a Christian from birth, even though I knew that wasn't possible. Still, he wasn't very "churchy" until he became a teenager and joined the large and dynamic youth group at a nearby church. Suddenly he was going to Bible studies and prayer meetings many times each week. One day he asked if I had noticed any changes in his behavior. As I said, Bart was always a good kid, but when he asked me that question, I realized he had been extra good of late, carefully noticing when I needed help or a word of encouragement. That's what I told him too. "Good," he said firmly. "Because I'm a Christian now, and I would hate it if that didn't make a difference."

I didn't know Tony as a little boy, but being a Christian was certainly making a difference in his life when we met in college. I was dazzled by my husband before I married him. Truth is, I still am. Tony has always been "on fire for Jesus," and even as a young man, he was a brilliant speaker who used his gifts to tell other people about the Jesus in whom he believed. As the years went by, it became also a very important part of Tony's preaching and teaching to tell people about the Kingdom of God and how all of us were called to join God in changing this world into what God intended it to be.

I confess that I often hoped Tony had enough faith for both of us, because a great deal of the time I was not sure if I was a Christian or not. I didn't feel the things Tony and many of our friends said they felt, nor did I ever hear God speaking to me. Sometimes, however, the whole story of God's grace seemed quite wonderful to me, and as I fell in love with Tony Campolo, I told myself I was a believer. Yet, if I am honest, I know I literally wished some of those "believing" times into my life because I knew that only a Christian could be Tony's wife.

After we married, and Tony learned more about my doubts, he gave me some very good advice. If I lived the way I thought a Christian would live, he told me, God would surely meet me there. So I tried my best to be a good pastor's wife, truly caring for our congregation, and especially finding meaning in visiting the elderly ladies who could no longer get out to church.

Tony was right. God did meet me—in the hospital room of a dear older lady I had come to love. Helen was frightened because she knew she was dying, and in my desperation to help her, I asked God to help me. The Holy Spirit came into that room and guided me to help my friend know God's grace and be assured of heaven. Jesus Christ has been real to me ever since that day. What I deeply regret is that that day came far too late for my children to have been raised by a truly authentic Christian mother. My son was nineteen and off at college when Jesus became a real part of my life.

Even as a doubter, I was always thankful when Tony took Bart along with him on ministry trips, and as parents we were delighted to see our son develop many of the same gifts his father had when it came to speaking in front of a congregation. Bart learned from his father about helping people to know who Jesus was, and it seemed to follow quite naturally that Bart began to do the very same kind of ministry. Of course, our son had his own set of gifts too. Bart was a great preacher from an early age, but he also cared very much about individuals who were hurting and instinctively knew how to relate to people who were poor or on the margins of society.

Tony and I were thrilled when Bart married a wonderful woman who shared his love and concern for people who needed it. I cannot count the many vulnerable people Bart and Marty invited to live in their home and to whom they gave hours and hours of loving care. They changed the lives of many—some of them folks I admit I would have had a very hard time inviting to live in my home.

Unlike Tony, who explains in this book how he saw Bart's faith ebb away over a period of time, I was completely shocked when Bart told us that he no longer believed in God. After all, God is love, and I still saw my son loving people as well or better than anyone I had ever known. I was deeply saddened as our conversations made it clear to me that in Bart's mind, God had no part in his ministry or in the rest of his life.

What convinces me of how serious Bart is about not believing in God is the fact that admitting it has made his life almost impossibly difficult. All of the places where he had worked, spoken, and run conferences were *Christian* places. He is no longer able to lead or work at any of them. Practically speaking, at just over fifty years of age, my son finds himself having to start his professional life all over again.

Of course, since his deconversion has become public, Bart has come under criticism from many Christians, which makes me angry. What exactly would these folks have him do? Would they like him to live a lie for the rest of his life, or at least until his parents are dead and gone? Well, Tony and I certainly wouldn't want that. There would be no way that we could share our hearts and our own deeply felt beliefs with Bart if he were less than honest with us. I am proud of Bart for being an authentic secular humanist when pretending to still be a Christian would have been a whole lot easier.

If not for Bart's honesty, this book would not exist. Nor would it exist unless Tony wanted more than anything to keep his close relationship with the son he loves unconditionally.

If you are wondering why I am not consumed with fears for Bart, or why I still find so much about my son to celebrate, it is because I believe with all my heart that the God I know in Jesus Christ is still very involved in Bart's life, just as God was part of my life a long time before I fully realized it. For me, that is true, even if it does not feel true for Bart right now.

Unlike me, my dear husband has lived all of his life with a consciousness of the presence of the living God. That is why it is so difficult for Tony to imagine his son living without this presence that is so dear to him and so much a part of who he is. I am thankful that Tony's God-consciousness kept him from saying any hurtful words on the night our son told us he did not believe in God, and that it keeps Tony from replying with bitterness when "friends" take it upon themselves to suggest that something wrong with his own faith or the way he has lived his life is the real reason our son is no longer "walking with the Lord."

Obviously, I wish Bart was still in ministry alongside his father, with a shared faith in Jesus Christ. But that isn't the way it is in our family, and I am proud of both Tony and Bart for working so hard to tell their story honestly, in the hope that doing so will help other parents and children who find themselves on opposite sides of faith. I pray for them both, and I believe God is at work in both their lives.

An Unusual Thanksgiving

by Tony Campolo

I'M A LIFELONG FOLLOWER of Jesus, a prominent evangelical preacher, and an emeritus professor of sociology at a Christian university. So then, it is difficult if not impossible to describe how I felt on Thanksgiving evening in 2014 when, in the dimly lit living room of his old three-story house in a severely "at-risk" Cincinnati neighborhood, my middle-aged son, Bart, told his mother and me that he no longer believed in God.

The whole experience was surreal. At first I did not believe what I was hearing, undoubtedly because I did not want to believe it. After all, this was my beloved son, who for more than two decades had been my partner in Christian ministry. Bart had always been my closest confidant and best adviser whenever I faced the difficult circumstances and decisions that invariably arise when ministering to poor and oppressed people in urban America and in third-world countries. We had prayed and worked together, and as a team we brought hope and help to places where it was desperately needed.

Like me, Bart was an itinerant preacher, boldly proclaiming a holistic gospel that combined the good news of God's salvation through faith in Christ with a plea for justice on behalf of the socially disinherited. Over the years, he had called tens of thousands of teenagers and young adults to turn away from the allurements of our consumeristic society and join in a revolution that could change the world from the mess that it is into the paradise for all that God wills for it to be.

In my own travels, I had met many college students whose lives had been transformed through my son's preaching and teaching. Again and again I encountered ministers and missionaries who told me that they would not be in Christian work had it not been for Bart. Countless individuals spoke to me in glowing terms of how Bart's loving counsel had carried them through spiritual struggles and rescued them from despair. So how could I reconcile all that with the news I heard on that fateful evening, that somewhere along the way Bart had lost his own faith in God?

It overwhelmed me. I hurt terribly.

I don't remember very much of what my wife Peggy or I said as Bart talked to us that night. Bart had, of course, prepared for what he would tell us, but we were completely unprepared for that kind of conversation.

When we were alone in our room later on, Peggy told me that as we listened to Bart, she had been praying silently that my pain wouldn't cause me to say something I might regret for the rest of my life. I am thankful that I did not, but I felt bewildered and unsure.

"What do we do now?" I asked my wife.

She did not hesitate for even a moment.

"Look," she said. "I've spent the past thirty years of my life telling the parents of gay and lesbian kids that as Christians, the only thing any of us can do is to accept and love our kids unconditionally, just as they are. I am certainly not about to do anything else when it comes to our own son."

Peggy made it quite clear that there was no way Bart would lose his mother's support and love, even if she wished with all her heart that things could be as we had thought they were just hours before. My own heart was breaking, and I was already dreading the questions I knew would be asked by both my friends and those who were not my friends, but in that moment I knew that there was no way Bart was going to lose the unconditional love of his dad, either.

Our son had already let us know how much he loved us and how much he regretted that his honesty was bound to hurt us. Nobody was angry. Nobody was bitter. I wasn't sure how, exactly, but I trusted that we would survive this crisis, as a family, so long as Peggy and I depended on God to help us manage whatever was still to come. All we could do that night was pray.

Once the initial shock wore off, I quickly realized that I could not and would not passively acquiesce to my son's declaration that he had left the Christian faith and adopted secular humanism as his new religion. I decided that I would reach out to Bart and ask him to provide answers to the most important questions that were racing through my mind. *What was it that had changed my son? Was there anything I could do to get Bart to reconsider his decision and come back to Christ and the Christian community? Had I failed to model for him a Christian lifestyle that was truly consistent with the teachings of Jesus? Was his departure somehow my fault?*

This last question troubled me even more when an editorial

in *Christianity Today,* America's foremost evangelical publication, suggested that if I had not focused so much on social issues and on my concerns for the poor, Bart's departure from Christianity might not have occurred. That article really hurt, because it made me doubt that I had been a good father.

These were only a few of the questions to which I desperately needed answers. Fortunately, there would soon be plenty of time for the two of us to talk. Shortly after my son announced his loss of faith, I booked a weeklong speaking tour in England, and Bart enthusiastically agreed to go with me. We both knew we would have many hours of conversation during the downtimes between my speaking engagements, and Bart seemed as eager to explain himself as I was to hear what he had to say. I prayed long and hard that during our conversations I would say things that would help bring him back to faith. He, on the other hand, wanted to help me understand what had led him away from Christianity and why he was still excited about his future. This book grew out of those conversations.

As we talked with each other in a succession of English parks and cafes, Bart and I became very aware that we were sharing our innermost feelings and expressing our most deeply felt convictions. We also realized that what we were saying to each other might be helpful to other individuals struggling with these issues, and especially to parents and children who found themselves at the same religious and intellectual impasse. After all, for most of us there is no safe place to discuss the difficult issues of faith or to work through doubts and questions. It required no special revelation for the two of us to understand that, in an age in which more and more young people answer questionnaires about religious affiliation by checking off "none," honest, respectful conversations like ours need to be happening between parents and children everywhere.

The world doesn't need any more theological polemics or debates about the truth of Christianity, and this book certainly isn't trying to be either of those. That said, certainly I am always trying to make my best case for following Jesus. If you are struggling with questions and doubts regarding the Christian faith, part of my job here is to answer those questions as well as I can and to provide the best possible answers for why I think Christians should stay in the fold. While I understand that Bart's faith probably won't be restored by my arguments, I hope they at least help him stay open to what ultimately must be the work of the Holy Spirit. I also hope that my arguments will model for other Christians a way to keep talking with our nonbelieving loved ones that is entirely loving and respectful without compromising the Gospel.

Now it is time for Bart to tell you what he told his mother and me on that fateful Thanksgiving night in Cincinnati, so we can all start this conversation together.

How I Left: A Son's Journey Through Christianity

by Bart Campolo

You can't really understand why I left Christianity unless you understand why I joined up in the first place. Of course, because my father is a famous evangelist, people often act as though I was a true believer on the day I was born, but the fact is that I didn't become a Christian until I was a sophomore in high school. Even then, it wasn't Tony Campolo who led me to Jesus.

Don't get me wrong—I wasn't some rebellious preacher's kid who refused to go to church because I hated my father for being such a hypocrite. On the contrary, my dad was my hero. I loved tagging along on his many speaking engagements. He wasn't going to many glamorous locations back then, but he made those trips extra fun by taking me to a movie or a nearby auto race on the way home. Even so, as far as I was concerned, the main attraction was watching my father mesmerize congregations with his jokes, his poignant stories, and above all, his passion for Jesus.

Honestly, for as long as I can remember, I've been a huge Tony Campolo fan. As a kid, even after I'd heard all his best sermons a dozen times, I still laughed, cried, and felt inspired along with the rest of the crowd. Then, when everyone else was treating him like a rock star afterward, I would proudly stand beside him and bask in the limelight. Best of all, he wasn't a phony. As far as I could tell, the things he preached about lined up with the way he lived. Trust me, it wasn't my father who kept me from becoming a Christian sooner. He made following Jesus seem like a noble adventure, and I always knew his faith was sincere. No, my problem was that I simply didn't believe in God.

Not that it bothered me much. Sure, pretending to accept all those Sunday school stories at face value and acting as though heaven and hell were real places felt strange, but I was a nice kid and I didn't want to embarrass or upset anyone, so I held my tongue. Things might have been different if I'd had to play-act about having faith at home too, but in general, our family didn't operate that way. From the beginning, my older sister, Lisa, made no bones about being largely uninterested in Christianity, and she's never wavered on that note. More importantly, although my mother grew up a minister's daughter before becoming a minister's wife, I think it's fair to say that she didn't really believe in God, either, when Lisa and I were growing up.

My mom is a sincere believer now, but her late-blooming faith is another story entirely. What matters here is that until I converted to Christianity in high school, our little nuclear family was surprisingly secular, by a regular vote of three to one. My dad occasionally tried to introduce daily devotions at breakfast, or family prayers before bedtime, but such initiatives were always unenthusiastically received and mercifully short-lived. Mom, Lisa, and I always came along when he preached locally, but when Dad was out of town, we generally took turns inventing reasons not to go to church. The rest of us respected his Christianity, both publicly and privately, but supernatural faith was his thing, not ours. In our family, the real religion was kindness. As long as I was nice—and especially nice to people on the margins—I was fine. Really, it was as simple as that.

Fortunately, being nice came easily to me, partly because I've always liked other people and partly because I enjoyed all the positive feedback I got from it, especially from my mother. Over and over again she would set me a challenge—make this lonely old lady laugh, invite that awkward kid over to play, help rescue this injured animal—and then shower me with praise when I met it. "Don't you feel good now?" she would ask afterward, and the truth was that I did.

By the time I reached high school, however, I felt even better about being athletic and popular, especially after I became the starting goalkeeper on the varsity soccer team as a sophomore. Suddenly I was invited to all the big parties, and pretty girls who'd never noticed me before began smiling in my direction. All the attention was fun, but I didn't much trust it. Instead, as the season wore on I became increasingly aware that my new status as a big man on campus had virtually nothing to do with my character. So then, in a spiritual sense, I was ripe for the picking.

I should have been suspicious when the confident, handsome senior I'd displaced as the starting goalie began showing a special interest in me, but I wasn't. I took it in stride when, rather than being bitter, Joel became my biggest booster, encouraging me at practices and cheering me on during the games, even though I'd stolen his thunder. I never wondered why he was cultivating me as a friend, even when he invited me to tag along to his church youth group's Thursday night meeting. Then, once we got there, I was too excited to care.

First, picture three hundred teenagers from a dozen nearby high schools packed into a carpeted multipurpose room, greeting one another with hugs, warmly welcoming newcomers, dividing into teams for high-energy group games, and then streaming into a darkened auditorium with cool videos playing on a huge screen while a live band plays loud rock and roll, after which a hip young adult gets up to give a short talk about what it means to be a true friend when someone's in trouble. Then picture those same kids—an uncommon assortment of jocks, cheerleaders, nerds, stoners, marching-band kids, and social outcasts—happily milling around together after the meeting, talking about their upcoming service project. Whether or not you can see it, I sure could: Joel's youth group was absolutely perfect for me—a huge, high-octane club for nice teenagers who genuinely enjoyed making things better for other people. I was hooked from day one, and over the next few months, that youth group quickly became the main focus of my life.

Of course, it didn't take long for me to figure out that the whole enterprise was built around the same kind of evangelical Christianity I'd been exposed to—and unconvinced by—for as long as I could remember. Joel and his friends weren't nominal believers, either; they were serious about their faith, in a way I'd never seen high school kids be serious about anything. They got up early to pray, held Bible studies in the cafeteria, sang gospel choruses on their way to the movies, and held each other accountable for everything from memorizing passages of scripture to maintaining their sexual purity. What stood out most to me, however, was the sincerity of their love for one another and the depth of their commitment to reaching out and drawing others into their circle of care. I still didn't believe in God, but for the first time in my life I really wanted to, not because I was afraid of going to hell, but rather because I wanted to become a full member of the most heavenly community I'd ever seen.

That's exactly what happened, of course. In the beginning I just went through the motions of being a Christian, but in the midst of that many ardent believers, it was only a matter of time before I began believing myself. We human beings are super-naturalists by nature, after all, especially when we're socially and emotionally motivated in that direction. The more I sang along with all those gospel choruses, the more I meant what they said. I still had my doubts about the Bible, but they were no match for my certainty about those transcendental experiences and my new friends' lifestyle of love. So then, a few months later, when Joel sat me down at a McDonald's and invited me to receive Jesus Christ as my personal Lord and Savior, I didn't hesitate.

I don't remember exactly when I discovered that Joel, at the direction of our youth group's adult leaders, had actually targeted me as a potentially valuable recruit and intentionally befriended me for that purpose, but that knowledge didn't bother me a bit. On the contrary, I was flattered. Of course, by that time I was being taught to target kids for evangelization myself, either because they clearly needed the kind of warm community we had to offer, or because, like me, they were popular, relationally gifted potential leaders who could help us draw in others. So then, from the very beginning, I understood that following Jesus wasn't so much about earning a ticket to heaven as it was about systematically transforming the world for the better by intentionally winning people over, one by one.

For a high school kid like me, becoming an evangelical Christian was a psychological bonanza. At just the moment when I was trying to figure out who I was and where I fit in, along came Joel's youth group offering me a ready-made identity that answered both of those questions and more. Suddenly I knew who I was with respect not only to God but also to the rest of the group, and really, the rest of the world. I soon had designated mentors on one hand and, on the other, a handful of younger believers I was charged with inculcating with Christian values even as I was learning those values myself. Together we learned to regard everyone outside our faith as potential converts whose immediate well-being and ultimate destiny was absolutely our responsibility.

Most of all, I relished being part of what felt to me like a revolutionary movement. I had always cared about helping other people, but evangelical Christianity focused my sense of mission in a powerful way and demanded that I order the rest of my life around it. In a very real sense, I was taught that God—and in particular your work on behalf of God—should figure into each and every decision, from what kind of music you liked (hint: it should be about God) to what time you woke up in the morning (hint: early enough for at least thirty minutes of Bible reading and prayer), to how many times you masturbated each week (hint: aim for zero). Burdensome as that may sound, finally knowing exactly how to be a good person felt strangely liberating to me, despite the fact that my friends and I could never fully pull it off. After all, even as novice Christians, we were already changing the world for the better simply by bringing more people into the fold.

Here's the thing: As much as I loved my new identity and lifestyle, from the very beginning I struggled with the Christian narrative around which they revolved. While everything evidently made perfect sense to my fellow believers, to me, both the Old and New Testaments seemed chock-full of problems. Indeed, my occasional experiences of spiritual transcendence during prayer meetings or group worship felt more reliable to me than much of what I found in the Bible. From the creation story in Genesis to the resurrection of Jesus, all the way through to the apocalyptic prophesies of Revelation, I found large swaths of scripture to be practically unbelievable. I know some folks are drawn to traditional religions by their divine revelations and miracle stories, but for me, the supernatural aspects of Christianity were always the price of admission, not the attraction.

Of course, all those revelations and miracle stories in the Bible might not have seemed so unbelievable to me if I had seen anything like them happening in my own world. Unfortunately, even on those occasions when divine intervention was most clearly called for, I saw no such thing. These days, people often ask exactly when I lost my faith, as though there were a single moment when the scales fell from my eyes. But the truth is that my Christian orthodoxy, and eventually my ability to believe in anything supernatural, actually died the death of a thousand cuts—and ten thousand unanswered prayers—over the course of more than thirty years.

The first of those "cuts" happened almost immediately, when a few college students from my new church invited me to join them in running a Christian summer day camp in Camden, New Jersey. Given my new priorities, I eagerly accepted, having no clue whatsoever about where we were going or what we were going to do. It wasn't until we drove into the neighborhood on the first day that I realized that we four bright-eyed would-be missionaries were in way over our heads.

In the late 1970s, Camden was a classic inner-city ghetto. Crack cocaine was just hitting the streets, and signs of destruction were everywhere. It wasn't just the boarded-up houses, broken-down cars, and graffiti that scared me, but also the hard-looking young men on the corners and the hollowed-out junkies pushing their shopping carts down the block. When we got out of the car to pass out flyers door-to-door, I wondered if any of us would return in one piece, and even if we did, I was absolutely sure nobody would show up for our day camp. By the next morning, however, we were alive and well and there were nearly a hundred kids waiting in the church parking lot a full hour before we opened the door for breakfast.

As you can imagine, the rest of that summer was pure chaos. For four hours each day it felt like all I did was yell "No!," "Stop!," and "Be quiet!," though surely I told plenty of Bible stories, led plenty of songs and games, and helped kids with plenty of arts and crafts projects as well. Honestly, I recall very little about our day camp programming, except that almost none of it worked the way my older friends and I had planned. Instead, what stands out in my memory are the precious, sparkling little boys and girls I fell in love with that summer, and the incredible confusion I felt as I began to realize what they were up against.

Inexperienced as I was as an urban missionary, I've always had a knack for cross-cultural friendships, and these kids were eager to tell me their stories. I had never before been touched by poverty, street violence, drug addiction, police brutality, or sexual abuse, but here it all was, being poured out daily on or in front of the innocent children in my day camp. This is not the place to describe those realities, but suffice it to say, they utterly changed me. By the time I left Camden to begin my junior year of high school, I was determined to spend the rest of my life making things better for people—and especially for children— stuck in hard places like that.

Clear as I was about my calling, however, my new faith was rocked by the suffering I'd seen in the lives of our day camp kids and their families, which called into question everything I was learning about God. One encounter in particular summed up my struggle, and try as I might, I couldn't put it out of mind. Toward the end of the summer I'd gotten to know Shonda, the warm, friendly mother of one of my favorite campers, a rambunctious ten-year-old named Craig. Given my "fresh convert zeal," it was only a matter of time before I tried to lead her to Christ, but when I did, she cut me off cold. "Don't waste your breath, Bart," she told me in a bitter voice. "I appreciate what you're trying to do here, but I don't want to hear about the love of God. You keep that mess away from me." Her response surprised me until I pressed her to explain.

Shonda had grown up in a Christian family, she told me, and loved everything about church until one day, as she walked home from school as a nine-year-old, a group of young men dragged her into a vacant house and gang-raped her. A few days later, when Shonda asked why God hadn't rescued her, her Sunday school teacher explained that because God was all-knowing and all-powerful, he could have stopped the attack, which meant that he must have allowed it for a good reason. The real question, the teacher went on, was what Shonda could learn from the experience that would enable her to better love and glorify God. In that moment, Shonda told me, she rejected God forever.

Unfortunately, my theology at the time wasn't much different from that of Shonda's Sunday school teacher. Indeed, I believed that God was sovereign, and that anyone who didn't accept Jesus in this life was going to hell afterward, which made God seem like the cruelest of tyrants, at least as far as Shonda was concerned. To me it was absurd to think that an all-powerful, all-loving God would willingly fail to protect an innocent little girl in this life, and then, when she couldn't trust Jesus as a result, doom her to eternal damnation in the life to come. So absurd, in fact, that I decided to think otherwise.

First of all, I decided that God wasn't actually in control of everything that happened in this world after all, and then I decided that there must be some kind of back door to heaven reserved for good people who didn't manage to come to Jesus before they died. I didn't come out and say all that right away, of course; it took many years for me to carefully work out my arguments and find the right Bible verses to support them. For better or worse, dialing down God's sovereignty and dialing up His mercy was simply a gut reaction to Shonda's story. In other words, for the first time in my Christian life, without consulting either my youth leaders or my Bible, I instinctively and quietly adjusted my theology to accommodate my reality.

I didn't know it then, of course, but that was the beginning of the end for me. Over the next thirty years, the realities of my life forced one theological accommodation after another, until there was literally nothing left of my evangelical orthodoxy. For instance, at Haverford College it was my two gay roommates.

The students I work with these days can hardly imagine it, but anyone who lived through the early 1980s will remember that back then there were very few places where homosexuality was openly discussed, let alone accepted and protected. At Haverford, though, things were different. There, for the first time, I grew close to people who, over the previous three years, I had come to understand as the most pitiable of sinners. I aimed to convert them, of course—in every sense of the word—but to do that, I knew I had to actually know and love them first. Of course, by the time that happened, I was the one who'd changed. For a while I struggled to reconcile the Bible's clear injunctions against homosexual behavior with my dawning realization that my gay friends' sexual orientations were no more chosen than my own. In the end, however, none of my interpretive "solutions" truly satisfied both my friends and my evangelical sensibilities, and I knew I had to choose between them.

Later, as a youth pastor in Minneapolis, Minnesota, I met and married Marty Thorpe, who was working as a live-in counselor at a faith-based women's drug rehabilitation center a few blocks from our church. Like my mother, Marty was a pastor's daughter who struggled with doubts of her own, and right from the start we found ourselves taking turns asking and trying to answer the hard questions, especially after we moved to Philadelphia to start our own ministry. I know many young couples find their faith strengthened by the process of having and raising children, but it didn't work that way for us. On the contrary, the older our kids got, the more we realized how uncomfortable we were about indoctrinating them with some of the most basic tenets of Christianity, despite the fact that by then both of us were fully engaged in recruiting Christian college students to organize evangelical day camps for inner-city kids all over town. Don't get me wrong—Marty and I were still very much believers at that point, and our shared commitment to Jesus's teachings about loving relationships, social justice, and community-building was actually growing stronger all the time. It was the content of our faith that kept shrinking, not its intensity.

Hell was long gone by then, of course, thanks to Shonda and a host of other Shondas we got to know. Biblical inerrancy was too, thanks to our gay friends. Later, as we saw one beloved child after another crushed by neglect and abuse, along with loving couples unable to conceive, young parents dying of cancer, and addicted friends relapsing—not to mention the destruction of poverty, war, and all kinds of natural disasters—despite our desperate prayers, the idea that God could do anything more than grieve with us slipped away too. We both always loved Jesus, of course—who doesn't, really?—but the more I thought about the Cross, the more I wondered why God couldn't just forgive us without killing anybody, the way He tells us to forgive one another. And if Jesus didn't need to die to save us, I went on, then maybe he didn't need to be born of a virgin or rise from the dead, either. Maybe he wasn't really divine at all, but just another good man whose followers got carried away after he died.

Again, none of this stuff happened quickly or all at once, and all throughout the process, Marty and I remained deeply committed to following the teachings of Jesus even as our confidence in their supernatural origins gradually eroded. I kept on preaching too, though over time my sermons were less about God's power and more about His love, which I increasingly conflated with our love for one another.

If this were an autobiography, I would describe in detail how Marty's and my little inner-city ministry in Philadelphia grew into a national organization called Mission Year, and how we led Mission Year for nearly fifteen years before I realized all that preaching and recruiting and organizing had carried me away from actually knowing the kinds of people who'd drawn me into it in the first place, and how Marty, our fourteen-year-old daughter, Miranda, and our eleven-year-old son, Roman, packed up and moved to Cincinnati so I could start all over again at street level.

Instead, I'll just tell you that almost as soon as we got to Cincinnati, we were surrounded by close friends who shared our most cherished values, and together we reached out and built a very fine intentional community in a very hard place. In the midst of that community, Miranda and Roman grew into young adulthood with incredible amounts of support and encouragement, and when we took custody of Roman's friend Corbin, our family became complete in a way none of us could have anticipated. Marty flowered as well, first as an artist and then as the manager of a truly terrific coffee shop near the University of Cincinnati, while I finally got to serve poor people as a relational minister in exactly the way I'd always dreamed about. Besides all that, we fell in love with the beauty, friendliness, and convenience of the city itself. Simply stated, Cincinnati was and is a terrific place to live, especially for an avid road cyclist like me.

Throwing my cycling into that last sentence might seem awkward, but trust me when I say it's a necessary transition. While I've always loved bicycles, I didn't begin riding seriously until a combination of basketball injuries and arthritis rendered both my ankles painfully unfit for almost any other form of exercise. Now I ride three or four times a week, often for fifty miles a ride, fully decked out in brightly colored spandex and hoping not to pass anyone I know. Los Angeles is a miserable city for that kind of riding, but in Cincinnati I didn't have to pedal very far away from the hustle and flow of our little ghetto to find myself alone on a country road, quietly rolling up and down the green hills of southwest Ohio or northern Kentucky. Ironically enough, it was on one of those lovely green hills, rather than in some dark and scary inner-city alley, that I almost died from clobbering my head in the summer of 2011.

I have no memory whatsoever of the bike crash that turned my life upside down. I remember getting dressed and leaving the house that morning, and I remember waking up in the hospital, but the hours in between are completely lost to me. As far as I know, I was going downhill on a freshly paved road when I lost control, skidded across the opposite lane, caught my front wheel in some soft dirt, and went airborne, flying headfirst into a tree at nearly forty miles per hour.

My helmet surely saved my life, but even so, I ended up with a pretty nasty concussion. For the first few hours, I didn't know how old my kids were or who the president of the United States was, and I repeated the same few conversations over and over again. For the next month or so, even after I got located on the basics, I wasn't myself at all. I thought more slowly and not as well. I couldn't remember simple things. I got headaches when I tried to read or watch television. I cried or became angry over little things. I couldn't concentrate on anything for very long. All I wanted to do was sleep. My doctor said all those symptoms were normal parts of the healing process, but I couldn't help worrying that I might not make it all the way back. So then, when I finally got there, I was much more than grateful.

I've always been an enthusiastic fellow, but after I recovered, every good thing in the world felt infinitely more wonderful to me. The food I ate tasted better. The air I breathed smelled sweeter. Each family member and friend I encountered seemed like a brand-new miracle of humanity. I loved falling asleep at night, and then I loved waking up the next morning. Reading and writing were fresh thrills to me. Hugging and kissing were off the charts. In a very real sense, I felt born again . . . again. This time, however, my mind was on this life only.

The more I thought about what had happened, the more I thought about the three big lessons from my bicycle crash. First and foremost, I learned that my core identity—my essential self, if you will—is all in my head. I don't mean that I'm a figment of my own imagination, of course, but rather that my individual personality, mind, heart, and soul are all contained in my brain. Simply stated, if something messes with my brain, it messes with who I truly am. I came to know this directly because, well, when my brain got smashed into a tree at forty miles per hour, my core identity changed in a hurry.

I probably should have figured that out about myself—and about everybody else—much sooner than I did. After all, I had already read enough popular science books like Malcolm Gladwell's *Blink* and David Linden's *The Compass of Pleasure* to know that both our judgments and our desires are largely controlled by the release and absorption of certain chemicals in our brains in ways our conscious selves only vaguely understand. Moreover, I had watched in dismay how after a close friend was miraculously healed from a massive brain tumor, he was so different in his abilities and appetites that neither he nor his family recognized him as the same person. *Which Chris would he be in heaven?* I wondered at the time. Still, after spending so many years preaching that only our bodies are mortal, I had stubbornly resisted the idea that our spirits might just be the same.

My second lesson was even simpler. I had always known it in theory, but after escaping death by just the thin plastic and Styrofoam margin of my bicycle helmet, I suddenly knew it in a deep and immediate way: I am going to die, and most likely too soon at that.

It was the third lesson, however, that brought the other two and everything else into focus for me: When my all-too-imminent death finally arrives, the matter and energy that are my body—including my brain and the core identity it contains—will rather quickly be broken down, absorbed, and transformed by the rest of the universe, and yours truly, Bart Campolo, will vanish forever. Someday remarkably soon I will no longer exist in any way, shape, or form, just as I did not exist for all of the billions of years before I was born. Like it or not, this life is the only one I've got.

One of the moments I most clearly recall from just after my bike crash was when I told Marty what I'd been thinking. In one sense it wasn't much different from a thousand other conversations we'd had before, when one or the other of us was struggling with the logic of faith. People often ask Marty how my deconversion impacted her, as if it happened all at once or as if she hadn't been along for the ride, but the truth is that we've generally tracked together, pushing each other along at times, and pulling each other back at others. This time, however, I wondered if she might think I had crossed over to another trail.

Instead, the conversation went something like this:

"You know, Marty, I think whenever we die, we'll just be dead. I'm pretty sure this life is all there is."

"Yeah, I've pretty much been thinking that way for a long time now."

"Really?"

"Yeah, really."

"Well, that's good . . . isn't it?"

"I think so. Still, what are you going to do for a living now?"

"What do you mean?"

"Well, you can't very well stay a professional Christian if you don't believe in God."

And that was that.

Marty obviously took it in stride, but at that moment, the realization of my own finitude was both utterly terrifying and indescribably thrilling to me. On the one hand, as Marty observed, it immediately cleared away whatever was left of my Christian faith, for better or worse. Oh, I knew from some of my Jewish friends that it was possible to believe in a good and just God without believing in the eternality of our individual souls, but for a longtime evangelical like me, that didn't feel like a viable option. My basic understanding of divine justice utterly depended on the promise that everyone who had been cruelly cheated by sin in this world would be more-than-fully recompensed by God in the world to come. As far as I was concerned, if there was no afterlife, there was no good and just God, which reduced the teachings of Jesus to an odd mix of delusional metaphysics and commonsense wisdom about the benefits of virtue. And which made the rest of the universe seem a whole lot more frightening than it had before, now that I knew it wasn't rigged in my favor.

On the other hand, realizing that this life is all I have imme-diately generated within me an irresistible sense of urgency to figure out a new way to live it. Up to then I had always walked by faith, more or less, but suddenly I needed to learn to walk by sight, and not just for my own sake.

You see, later in that first conversation, Marty had asked me another question: "Do you want us to stay married, now that there's no God to punish us if we don't?" I was pretty sure she was kidding, but the question unnerved me just the same.

"I do," I replied quickly. "Don't you?"

"Absolutely," she said with a sly smile. "I find you very at-tractive." Then, as if it just occurred to her, she added, "But what about the kids? Do you still love our kids?"

"Of course I do, you silly woman!" I exclaimed.

"Good," she said, matter-of-factly, as if she were running through a checklist. "Me too. But what about the rest of it? Do we still want to reach out to poor people, now that we don't have to? Do we still care about building warm and welcoming communities? Are we still committed to social justice? How about education and the arts? Are we still convinced that sacri-ficial love is the best way of life?"

She already knew the answers to all those questions, of course, but she asked them anyway to drive home her point. Some things in our lives were going to be different from now on, but not the most important things. Christian or not, we were the same people, the same couple. Our worldviews had changed, but our most important values had not. The real ques-tion wasn't how we were going to live without God; we already knew that. The real question was how we were going to justify that lifestyle—to ourselves, to our kids, to our Christian friends, and especially to other people without faith—now that we could no longer claim to stand on the word of God.

That's the part that thrilled me, right from the start. As soon as I faced up to the fact that I no longer believed in Christianity—or any other kind of supernaturalism, for that matter—the first thing I wanted to do was work out a new philosophical foundation for a way of life that I already knew worked in practice. Maybe it was because I'd effectively functioned as an agnostic for a few years already, but it never occurred to me that life without God might have no meaning. On the contrary, among my first thoughts after my deconversion was this: *Holy mackerel! Evangelizing people to love, justice, and community is going to be a whole lot easier now that I don't have to convince them to buy a whole set of unbelievable Iron Age myths at the same time!* So then, almost as soon as my still-healing brain allowed, I went to the library and started reading up on the so-called New Atheists.

I'm telling my own story here, not trying to convince anyone else not to believe in God, so there's no need for me to summarize the various logical, scientific, and commonsense arguments of Richard Dawkins, Christopher Hitchens, Daniel Dennett, and Sam Harris. Suffice it to say that their reputations as religious debunkers, champions of science, and celebrators of the wonders of nature are well deserved, and that reading their books was tremendously helpful for me as an emerging secularist. One of those books in particular, Harris's *Letter to a Christian Nation,* was practically a word-for-word summary of my frustrations during my latter days as a believer, and a kind of primer for responding to the questions I am most commonly asked these days.

As much as I appreciated the New Atheists, however, I quickly realized that as excellent as they were at detailing the philosophical underpinnings of unbelief, challenging both the basis and the implications of various traditional theologies and religious practices, and arguing for more rational approaches to the problems of life, they had no interest in creating anything like a secular church. On the contrary, they were repelled by the content of traditional religion and by its form, and in particular by the specter of anyone intentionally indoctrinating or proselytizing anyone else into a different way of life. In this respect, they were and are like many members of the established secular community, who are still reeling from bad experiences with religion.

I was still living in the Walnut Hills neighborhood in Cincinnati, however, surrounded by neighbors in all kinds of trouble, and after nearly thirty years of youth ministry, I knew there were lots of people out there looking for guidance and inspiration. I understood and respected the integrity of the New Atheists' "live and let live" approach to outreach, but I couldn't adopt it for myself. As it turned out, my values weren't the only thing about me that hadn't changed; I was and still am an evangelist at heart. In the aftermath of my deconversion, scientific explanations and logical arguments weren't enough for me; I was looking for a new gospel.

Nonconformist pastor Edwin Paxton Hood once warned, "Be as careful of the books you read as of the company you keep; for your habits and character will be as much influenced by the former as the latter." In my case, it was the company I kept (my merrily atheistic pal Rich Stazinski) who gave me the book (*The Great Agnostic* by Susan Jacoby) that changed everything by introducing me not only to my new gospel—secular humanism—but also to my new hero—nineteenth-century politician and orator Robert Ingersoll. Before I knew it, my desk was covered by volumes of Ingersoll's countless speeches, articles, poems, eulogies, and letters, and all I could think was how lucky I am that history hadn't quite forgotten him before I was ready to appreciate his wit and wisdom.

Again, here is not the place for me to attempt a summary of Ingersoll, who was raised by a devout Christian minister before becoming one of the nation's most famous orators. In an era when public speeches were popular entertainment, Ingersoll drew huge crowds to hear his talks on science, abolitionism, Darwin's theory of evolution by natural selection, the separation of church and state, free speech, women's rights and equality, humanism and free thought, and the many shortcomings of the Bible, church, and preachers. By all accounts, including those of his enemies, he was warm, funny, passionate, and wildly entertaining. What struck me most when I started reading Ingersoll, however, was his deep and obvious commitment to love as the ultimate hope of humanity, and his great eloquence in communicating it. Better than anyone I've ever encountered, he put into words the idea that the surest path to true happiness is to concern yourself with the happiness of others. He instantly became my role model as a secular humanist evangelist.

Thanks to Ingersoll, it didn't take long for me to know what I wanted to do next, and thanks to Marty, I wasn't worried that doing it might cost me my marriage. I wasn't worried about losing my children, either, given the many conversations we'd had about religious differences over the years. My boys had been open about their own problems with Christianity for years, and while my daughter still dabbled in church stuff, she always made plenty of room for people who didn't. Likewise, while most of Marty's and my closest friends were still committed Christians, they had tracked with us through so many changes already that I was pretty sure they wouldn't reject us now. Honestly, my parents were the only ones I was really worried about telling. They'd been badly shaken up when Marty and I suddenly moved away from them to Cincinnati, and again when I'd finally stopped managing Dad's office a few years later, but I figured hearing this news would be an earthquake many orders of magnitude larger.

Every nonbelieving child of extremely religious parents dreads breaking those parents' hearts, some so much that they keep their truth to themselves, but that was never an option for me. It wasn't just that I could no longer work as a professional Christian, either, or that I was already plotting out my new career as a secular leader. The main reason I had to tell my parents was simpler: Over the years we've always been close, and I couldn't stand the idea of them not really knowing me anymore. Even so, it was bound to be tough.

I didn't think my parents were going to fly off the handle and disown me, of course. They might not like what I had to tell them, but it certainly wouldn't surprise them. Like everyone else, they'd watched my steady movement away from orthodoxy for a long time. I didn't think they'd condemn me to burn in hell, either. Their theologies don't work that way, and neither do their hearts. Instead, what I was counting on was lots of hand-wringing about my family's and my future and not a little bit of sadness about their own. After all, it's a pretty big story in evangelical circles—and an embarrassing one at that—when Tony Campolo's son loses his faith.

There wasn't anything we could do about the hit to my father's reputation in Christendom, or about all the difficult conversations both my parents surely faced once their extended families and friends found out, but in the days leading up to our first Thanksgiving as secular humanists, Marty and I thought long and hard about how to break our news to them as positively as possible. The key, we figured, was to talk as little as possible about what we no longer believed, and as much as possible about all the values and commitments we still had in common with them.

I'd recount that first conversation in detail if I could, but the only things I can remember clearly are my dad asking a handful of clarifying questions, and then sitting quietly with his head in his hand, my mom doing her best to stay upbeat in spite of his obvious dismay, and Marty's and my agreement afterward that they didn't seem to love or respect us one bit less than they had when we started. I'd probably remember more details if that had been our only conversation on the subject, but as this book clearly demonstrates, it was just the first of many, and lately they've all begun to run together in my mind.

There is one moment, however, which stands out to me. It happened toward the end of my dad's and my trip to England, during which we talked practically nonstop for an entire week about our contrasting worldviews, on a day when it seemed to me I'd gotten the best of the argument. Instead of being frustrated, however, my father seemed quite pleased. "You did very well today, Bart," he told me. "I don't agree with all you've said, but I'm really starting to understand you again!"

How I Stay: A Father's Story of Keeping the Faith

by Tony Campolo

As I read Bart's journey into faith and then, with great pain, the story of him drifting away from Jesus, I realize how eloquent and convincing my dear son can be. For better or worse, my story lacks that kind of drama and style. St. Paul wrote to the Christians in the city of Corinth that he lacked *"excellency of speech"* (1 Corinthians 2:1, KJV) and was devoid of *"enticing words of man's wisdom"* (1 Corinthians 2:4, KJV). I often feel the same way when I write, so I pray that God will help my readers go beyond my limitations and sense something of the reality of Jesus that I feel in the depths of my being. To that end, here is a brief sketch of how I came to be where I am as a Christian.

I grew up in the kind of household where God the Father, the Holy Spirit, and especially Jesus of Nazareth were every bit as real as every other member of the family. My mother's family had been rescued from poverty by a Baptist seminary student, and she and my two older sisters were enthusiastic churchgoers who had me singing gospel music on our local Christian radio station almost as soon as I was out of diapers. My father, an Italian immigrant who spoke very little English, worked long hours at the RCA factory, and we never had much money, but I was always well dressed for Sunday school, and my mother and sisters were absolutely convinced that God had big things in store for me. Every day as I left the house for school, I heard the same refrain: "Go over the top for Jesus, Anthony!" We sang hymns together, prayed together, and together experienced the joys of Christian fellowship. Frankly, I can't remember ever not loving and trusting the God my family introduced to me.

In the eighth grade, I became friends with a classmate named Burt, who shared my evangelical convictions, and we remained close throughout our high school years. It was Burt who introduced me to Bible Buzzards, a great group of young people who gathered every Saturday evening to sing gospel songs and study the Bible under the guidance of Tom Roop. Tom was a Christian layman who seemed to know the Bible inside and out, and his enthusiasm for the Gospel was utterly contagious. The impact that Tom had on me and the other teenagers who sat under his teachings is impossible to exaggerate. We all became zealous Christians who organized our lives around learning more about Jesus and sharing his story. Tom poured himself into each of the forty-plus teenagers who came together each week, and we looked to him as a kind of spiritual father. Given his passion for evangelism, it is no surprise that many of us became missionaries and pastors.

Of course, as my son, Bart, discovered for himself many years later, there's more to a good youth group than Bible study, and Christian conviction isn't only a matter of doctrinal correctness. Even now, while I can recite many arguments that give me good reasons for the hope that lies within me (1 Peter 3:15), my faith in Christ remains grounded in personal experiences that first began when I was a Bible Buzzard. I'm still a fairly good Christian apologist, but at the end of the day, I have to admit that the primary foundation of my faith is not what I know, but rather what I feel. As Blaise Pascal once observed, "The heart has reasons that reason will never know."

The Bible says in Romans 8:16 that God *"beareth witness with our spirit"* (KJV) that we are His children, and in the depths of my being I sense the presence of God's Holy Spirit doing just that. By the grace of God I have been given the gift of faith. Certainly there are times when this inner spiritual assurance wanes, but I consistently find deliverance from my doubts when I cry out like that desperate man who once asked Jesus to heal his son, *"Lord, I believe; help thou mine unbelief"* (Mark 9:24, KJV).

I can't remember when I did not accept the basic doctrines of the Christian faith, but before I met Burt and Tom, those doctrines were simply historical facts to me, not life-changing experiences. So then, while I cannot pinpoint exactly what an old hymn calls "the hour I first believed," I know it was during high school that I gradually came to realize my soul was hungry for something more than just salvation, and by the time I enrolled at Eastern Baptist College, the inner presence of Jesus had become for me an everyday conscious reality.

Sensing the presence of Jesus in my life should have made everything different for me, but it didn't. While I certainly sinned less often in conventional ways, I was not miraculously transformed into a sinless person, and indeed in some ways my growing "righteousness"—which in many cases was really self-righteousness—made me dangerous to other people. Indeed, as

I look back over the years, I see many times when I did worse than just fall short of that righteous way of living that the Bible calls *"the glory of God"* (Psalm 19:1). It was not simply that I continued breaking this or that prescribed law laid down in the scriptures; my sins hurt people. Indeed, the older I get and the more I think about that great and glorious day when all truth will be revealed as we account for our lives, the more I pray that those I have hurt will be able to show me the same kind of grace that Jesus has already.

Honestly, I don't think I could handle the burden of my guilt alone. When I sing the hymn "Amazing Grace," I resonate with the line that says, "'Twas grace that taught my heart to fear, and grace my fears relieved." It is usually in the still of the night that the Holy Spirit brings to consciousness the hurts my sins have caused, and it is during such times that I confess these sins to Jesus and *feel* the loving assurance of His grace.

I sometimes wonder how people like Bart, who no longer believe in the grace of God, handle their guilt. Perhaps, as Sigmund Freud suggested, they repress it by burying the memories of past sins deep within themselves. But Freud went on to explain that such repression doesn't really work in the long run, and that guilt always emerges from the subconscious, sometimes as phobias and sometimes as neurotic behavior. One of the main reasons I remain a Christian is because I love knowing that my sins are not only forgiven, but also forgotten! That they are, as scripture puts it, blotted out, buried in the deepest sea and remembered no more.

For me, the peace of heart and soul when I pray to God for forgiveness is absolutely necessary. As I confess my sins, I sense the crucified Jesus reaching out to me across time and space to absorb into Himself those dark and ugly realities that mar my sense of well-being. Hymns I have sung in churches a thousand times over the years have helped create this awareness of deliverance more than all the sermons that followed.

My sin, oh the bliss of this glorious thought,
My sin, not in part but the whole,
Is nailed to His cross, and I bear it no more,
Praise the Lord, praise the Lord, oh my soul.

—"It Is Well with My Soul," Horatio G. Spafford (1873)

Important as that basic gospel message was and continues to be to me, I will always be grateful to Eastern Baptist College and Seminary for broadening my early evangelical fundamentalism into a deeper understanding of the Christian faith that has, for me at least, stood the test of time.

The motto of the school, which has now become Eastern University, is "The Whole Gospel for the Whole World," and it was there that I learned I had been proclaiming only half the good news about Jesus. In class after class, I was taught that Jesus came into the world not simply to transform one individual at a time into what the Bible calls a "new creation," but also to initiate a global movement to change this world from what it is into what God wants it to be. According to my professors, this new world—the Kingdom of God—would be marked by justice and well-being for all people. In short, at Eastern I learned that receiving the Gospel wasn't just about accepting Jesus as your "personal savior" in order to go to heaven, but was even more about committing yourself to engaging and overcoming the principalities and powers of this world on behalf of those in need.

Of course, it wasn't just in my classes that my understanding grew. I also met and married Peggy at Eastern, and she taught—and continues to teach—me a great deal about the practical side of following Jesus's example. At the same time, first in college and later during seminary and graduate school, I began to serve Jesus by pastoring a variety of small churches in New Jersey and Pennsylvania. It was at one of those pastorates, the Upper Merion Baptist Church in King of Prussia, Pennsylvania, that my life's mission first came into focus.

Upper Merion Baptist was located less than a mile from the newly constructed national headquarters of the American Baptist Churches USA, the then two-million-member mainline denomination of which it was a part, so it wasn't surprising that a number of denominational leaders chose to be part of our church. Fortunately for me, one of those leaders was the brilliant and controversial Jitsuo Morikawa, the ABC's director of evangelism, who quickly befriended me. Both as a student and as a young pastor, I valued my friendship with Dr. Morikawa. Indeed, when I had to choose a dissertation subject for my Ph.D. degree at Temple University, I decided on the topic "A Sociological Analysis of the Structure and Function of the Church Within the American Baptist Churches" so that I could study Morikawa's ideas about evangelism. According to Morikawa, a major redefinition of the mission of churches and a major restructuring of their programs was required for them to successfully carry out their evangelistic mission. In the process of writing my dissertation, I read everything that Morikawa had published, in addition to having multiple personal conversations with him, and by the time I finished, my theology and my personal sense of mission had been transformed.

Ever since Bible Buzzards, evangelism had been my raison d'être. Wherever I went, I wanted everyone to accept Jesus, pray the Believer's Prayer, and be saved. As I wrote my dissertation, however, it became increasingly clear to me that evangelism was more than just leading people to have the kind of faith in Christ that would assure them of eternal life. With Morikawa's help, I came to realize that true evangelism also involved declaring the good news that Jesus was at work through His people, changing the world from what it is into what Jesus called the Kingdom of God. I began to see everywhere in scripture that this Kingdom of God was not simply in some otherworldly place where believers would go when they died, but was a reconstructed society here in *this* world, marked by love and justice.

Praying the Lord's Prayer took on new significance when I repeated the words *"Thy Kingdom come, Thy will be done <u>on earth</u>, as it is in heaven"* (Matthew 6:10, KJV). These words came to mean for me that His Kingdom was not just "pie in the sky when you die." It was a here-and-now kingdom for which I was praying. Of course, in order for this kingdom to come, individuals needed to be "saved" from their sinful natures, and social institutions as well. More and more, I began to consider how the political sector of society would have to be changed if it were to serve God's will on earth, and what the legal, economic, and educational systems would have to be like if they were to reflect God's will. Everything had to be restructured to reflect the will of God. Most of all, I realized that the injustices suffered by the poor and oppressed peoples of the world had to be challenged.

As I was going through this spiritual metamorphosis, what I read in scripture took on powerful new meaning. The parables of Jesus, I realized, were about the Kingdom of God and gave profound insights into how Kingdom people (that's who Christians are supposed to be) were to live and act in order to become God's agents of change. There was a new dawning in my heart and mind as I realized that by becoming a Christian, I was joining a revolutionary movement that could transform the world into the kind of society God wants for it to be.

All of these changes in my thinking were taking place during the early part of the 1960s wherein the American society was in turmoil as it dealt with the civil rights movement and the antiwar movement. It wasn't long before I felt God calling me to more fully participate. I was realistic about the politically conservative mind-set at Upper Merion Baptist, however, and realized that my becoming an activist in these controversial social movements might well tear our congregation apart. So then, as soon as teaching opportunities opened up for me at both Eastern University and the University of Pennsylvania, I decided to leave the pastorate.

I loved the classroom right from the start and quickly discovered that the academic community was the perfect setting in which to share my new vision of "holistic evangelism," which combined a traditional emphasis on personal discipleship with a deep commitment to social justice. It seemed like everywhere I turned, there were young men and women hungry for a form of religion that would channel their spiritual energies into practical activities that promised to make a difference for the future of the world. Enrollments in my classes, both at secular Penn and at highly evangelical Eastern, grew larger every year. These students wanted to hear my new vision and then join me in acting on it.

At Eastern, we organized teams of students to go into the government housing projects of Philadelphia to do after-school tutoring for inner-city children. A summer program was added, and soon we had hundreds of inner-city children participating in what we called "street camps," featuring sports, cultural enrichment activities, and Bible stories. Students from other colleges and universities soon joined in, and our programming quickly spread to other cities, and eventually to Haiti, the Dominican Republic, and other countries as well.

In these programs, there was always a strong emphasis on leading children and teenagers to put their faith in God, and over the years, thousands were won to Christ. At the same time, the college students who became involved were also being deeply changed by the experience. Today there are hundreds of pastors, missionaries, doctors, social workers, and other change agents who trace their callings back to those early days of inner-city ministry.

Of course, I was being changed as well. The more I became involved as an organizer, the more I felt Christ's presence among the poor and needy children my students and I were serving. Little by little, I came to believe, with great intensity, that there is actually a preference for the poor throughout the scriptures and that Jesus's good news is and must be especially good for those who are suffering under oppression. Evangelism for me became simply calling people to live out their commitments to Christ by working for justice, while at the same time bringing them to an understanding of personal salvation. It involved urging Christians to get down to the street to serve those people Jesus calls *"the least of these"* (Matthew 25:40), as though each of them were the Lord Himself. But even beyond that, it involved truly believing that He who is already at work through His followers will one day return and bring it all to glorious completion, when in fact *"The kingdoms of this world are become the kingdoms of our Lord, and of his Christ; and he shall reign forever and ever"* (Revelation 11:15).

It is that last part, my confidence in Jesus's ultimate victory over sin and death, that continues to sustain me, especially in times of trouble. You see, I have no utopian idealism to keep me going. I am now eighty-one years old and therefore inescapably aware that the end of my life is very near. Each morning as soon as I wake up, I thank God for another day wherein I can enjoy life in this wonder-filled world, but I know very well that for billions of people around the world, life is not so sweet. Honestly, if I did not believe that there was love and justice waiting on the other side of death, especially for those who are still suffering in this life, I think I would despair. As I sense the end of life rushing toward me, I lean on the awareness that Jesus is with me. He comforts me as I feel His words reverberating in my mind: *"I am the resurrection, and the life: he that believeth in me, though he were dead, yet shall he live"* (John 11:25). There are times when the Evil One (and yes, I do believe in that Satanic personage) haunts me with the thought that my belief in the eternal Kingdom of God is only wishful thinking, as Bart's new worldview suggests. But in those moments I say the name of Jesus over and over again within myself, and I experience Him driving my fears and doubts away.

Being a Christian is and has been, for me, a chance to be part of history's ultimate movement. All the work in various ministries that consumed so much of my time and energy along with my preaching over the years have been carried out in the context of this biblical vision of the Kingdom of God, which even now is breaking loose in the world. Those who want to mock me can easily say that I sound like one of the Blues Brothers, declaring, "I am on a mission from God," but it is this belief that has given form and meaning to my life. Following Jesus rescued me, once and for all, from becoming one of what T. S. Eliot calls "the hollow men," for whom the world will end not with a bang, but with a whimper because they have no hope. And trusting in Jesus continually delivers me from the cynicism growing up all around me, which concludes, in the words of Shakespeare, that life "is a tale told by an idiot, full of sound and fury, signifying nothing."

In a real sense, my life of faith has been an ongoing dialogue with God and with other Christians. I regularly realize that the Holy Spirit is alive and well within me when I pause to consider what I should say or do, either alone or in the company of other believers, with God in mind. For me, this is one of the meanings of prayer. Prayer for me is not just giving thanks before meals, or asking for guidance and divine intervention at designated times during the day. Above and beyond all that, I believe that prayer is what happens during those moments throughout the day when I feel God interacting with me, both directly and through other people, intentionally humanizing me by making me more and more like Jesus.

It is hard to explain what God's Spirit does *for* me and *to* me as I experience what otherwise might be mundane experiences and encounters. Somehow He creates within me a sensitivity to the wonders lurking within the ordinary people and things around me that some phenomenologists would call "mindfulness." He makes me hyperaware of the radiant blessings (I can't think of another word) that are everywhere around us, literally waiting to be acknowledged and enjoyed. Because of His indwelling presence I am truly able to "seize the day."

Spirituality for me means that everyday experiences and relationships can be enhanced if I just take time to stop and reflect on them with God in mind. The inner presence of Christ's spirit empowers me for this. When I am surrendered to His Spirit, I sense at times an ability to eternalize precious moments in time and make them part of my permanent, existential identity. When I am spiritually "turned on" in this way, the transience of a particular moment is interrupted so that something transcendent can come through it and stay with me. Honestly, I believe that if I were to live on this earth for a thousand years, the reality of those moments would nevertheless remain a vital part of who I am.

I am not denying that non-Christians can identify with what I am describing, but for me, this kind of awareness can be understood only as a gift from God. There may be other ways to be mindful of transcendence in the midst of the ordinary, but the only way I am sure of it is to acknowledge the Holy Spirit within me. As I listen to Bart wax eloquent about the wonders of life, he seems to me to be describing what social scientist Abraham Maslow called "peak experiences." When he talks this way, however, I often ask myself if he is really just encountering God. It just might be that what Bart has really rejected is not God, but rather the way so many of us Christians usually talk about God. Maybe it is our overly theological language, among other things, that has caused him and so many others to describe themselves as spiritual but not religious.

In any case, this brief survey of my spiritual development

should give you a working knowledge of how I came to be the kind of Christian I am today. There's much more to my story, of course, some of which will come out in the dialogue ahead. What matters most for now, I think, is to understand that while my Christian faith has a strong and certain theological basis, its true foundation is my long and ongoing experience of God's abiding presence in my life.

CAN'T, NOT WON'T: LOSING FAITH IS NOT A CHOICE

by Bart Campolo

As a humanist minister, my advice to newly deconverted Christians is always the same: When the time comes to break the news to your still-believing friends and family members, don't just tell them everything you no longer believe and why. Instead, begin the conversation by listing all the cherished values that you first learned in church, and all the teachings of Jesus you love most dearly, and all the important commitments to social justice and community building that your loved ones and you still share. Then, and only then, tell them why you can no longer believe as they do.

It's a more positive approach, of course, and often it sets the stage for a conversation more focused on common ground. Still, sooner or later, we post-Christians inevitably face the same big questions from those who remain faithful: What happened? What went wrong? Why does Christianity no longer make sense to you? Once again, my advice is always the same: Don't make a theological case; tell them your story.

Of course, I'm not suggesting that you need to work out your complete autobiography before you can let anyone else know that your mind has changed. On the contrary, my rule of thumb in these conversations is to boil down your reasoning into a handful of simple declarative statements, and then use as few words as possible to explain each one. My main point here is only that those few words should be as personal as possible. In short, the kindest, safest way to describe where you are, spiritually speaking, is to simply explain how you got there.

Looking back, I wish I'd had a humanist chaplain to give that advice to me. Beginning with my parents that Thanksgiving night in Cincinnati, and for some time afterward, I often made the mistake of listing all my problems with Christianity first, which always put my believing counterparts on the defensive. I didn't actually want to spoil anybody else's faith, but starting off by attacking the veracity of the Bible, the morality of the Cross, and the historical record of the church sure made it seem that way. Eventually, however, I learned to just cut to the chase: For reasons beyond my control, I simply stopped believing in God. The rest are just details.

It would be different, of course, had I switched from Protestant to Catholic or Greek Orthodox, or jumped all the way over to Judaism or Islam, or even farther to Hinduism, Mormonism, Scientology, or any number of other supernatural religions. In any of those cases, the particulars of my theology—and especially my understanding of scriptural authority—would be much more relevant. In my case, however, all that really matters is that over many years my ability to believe in any kind of supernatural reality gradually faded away, until I finally became convinced that the natural universe—matter, energy, and time—is all that exists.

Not surprisingly, that kind of naturalism didn't come naturally to me. On the contrary, I spent most of my adult life actively fighting off the idea that God is a human invention rather than the other way around. Practically from the moment I became a Christian, I was routinely plagued by existential doubts, most of which I didn't so much resolve as bury in order to get on with my life. It wasn't just my career that depended on not facing up to the question of God. My personal identity, my public image, my marriage, my family relationships, and my closest friendships were all built around trusting and proclaiming Jesus as our risen Lord and Savior. Thanks to a last-minute intervention by my mother when I was a teenager, there wasn't a huge cross tattooed across my back, but there might as well have been. My entire life was wrapped up in the Gospel. Really, I can't imagine anyone being more motivated than I was to keep the faith.

Even so, I couldn't do it. Please, stop for a moment and read that last sentence again, because this point is very important. I didn't *choose* not to believe in God; I just stopped believing. Abandoning the Christian narrative wasn't a joyous, willful decision, but rather the unhappy conclusion of a long battle against all evidence to the contrary. Like so many other post-Christians, I didn't manufacture my own deconversion on purpose; it happened to me. Slowly but surely, that benevolent presence that once seemed absolutely real to me felt like an imaginary friend instead. I never turned my back on God; He disappeared before my eyes.

Don't get me wrong—I'm not saying my long-standing issues with the Bible, central Christian doctrines of original sin and substitutionary atonement, and the checkered history of the church—not to mention a long litany of unprevented tragedies and unanswered prayers—had nothing to do with it. I'm not saying mounting scientific evidence and logical arguments for naturalism by secular writers such as Richard Dawkins and Sam Harris didn't eventually influence me as well. All I'm saying is that that stuff isn't what undid me. Like my father and every other true believer, I found ways to work around all those problems and more as long as I knew for a fact that God was real.

Here is an example. Back in college, I signed up for a course with Dr. James Barr, a highly distinguished biblical scholar from Oxford. Because Dr. Barr had come to the United States primarily to do research, that course, The Scope and Authority of the Bible, wasn't widely advertised. In fact, besides my good friend Jerry and me, only two other students enrolled.

I doubt it was Dr. Barr's intention to radically challenge my relationship with God, but as soon as we started reading his now-classic book *Fundamentalism,* I felt completely under siege. His weekly lectures were even more unsettling. Speaking in his friendly Scottish brogue, Dr. Barr briskly walked my classmates and me through the Old and New Testaments, casually pointing out a wide array of errors, internal contradictions, and morally repugnant passages along the way, and inviting us to reconsider how and why they got there. I had never looked at the Bible that way, and when I did, the results were devastating.

Oddly enough, the biblical inconsistency that made the biggest impression on me then had nothing to do with the slavery, misogyny, and genocide that so troubled me later on. Instead, what really got under my skin were the clear discrepancies between the descriptions of Paul's conversion in Acts 9 (where everyone hears Jesus's voice but only Paul sees the blinding light and falls to the ground), Acts 22 (where everyone sees the light but only Paul hears Jesus and falls), and Acts 26 (where everyone see, hears, and falls together). How was it, I wondered, that five years into a Christian journey in which literally everything depended on our holy scripture being utterly flawless, I had never noticed such an obvious and incontrovertible flaw?

There were more flaws where that came from, of course, and Dr. Barr was only too happy to share them with us. Before long, I was seriously questioning everything I'd been taught about the Bible. My friend Jerry was troubled too, and the two of us often talked late into the night, desperately searching for ways to hang on to the biblical foundation on which our lives were built. We knew the God who met Paul on the Damascus road was real, after all; we'd both felt that same overwhelming presence ourselves.

Suspecting that behind all that academic rigor, Dr. Barr was also a believer, we thought he might be willing to help us. When we went to see him, however, Barr deftly deflected our more personal questions and offered no spiritual guidance whatsoever, even though Jerry and I were clearly in distress. As our professor, Barr explained, it wasn't his place to provide pastoral care. On our way out, however, the old man threw us a bone. With a twinkle in his eye, he quietly suggested we might enjoy writing our final papers about German theologian Karl Barth's approach to biblical authority.

As a Christian, I used to happily explain how Karl Barth rescued my faith by showing me how to strongly affirm the divine inspiration of the Bible without pretending it isn't shot through with human errors. What makes the Bible authoritative, according to Barth, is not its historical accuracy or literary perfection, but rather the fact that God consistently uses it to hold together and guide his people. For Barth, the Bible is only a sign that points to the true Word of God, who always was and is Jesus Christ. It is holy because God Himself has chosen to speak through it to dynamically communicate His will to His church.

I then used to describe the joyful relief I felt when, across from Jerry at a library table covered by dusty volumes of Barth's incredibly massive *Church Dogmatics,* I realized I could stay a Christian after all, and the happy surprise when I called home to tell my dad, only to discover that he'd named me Bart (short for Barth) because those books rescued his faith too, way back when he was in seminary.

Nowadays, though, I have mixed feelings about Professors Barr and Barth, because together they helped keep me an evangelical Christian long after I otherwise would have given it up. The upside of their theological enabling was all the wonderful relationships and experiences I enjoyed as a believer. The downside, of course, was that I continued to build my life—and eventually my career—on a biblical foundation whose first cracks hadn't really been fixed at all, only patched over.

Why didn't I recognize the very complicated theological gymnastics Barth was doing in order to protect the Bible from its own mistakes? Why didn't I immediately see that all he'd really given me was a clever way to work around everything from flat-earth references and internal contradictions to clear scriptural allowances for slavery, misogyny, genocide, homophobia, and anti-Semitism? Why was I so willing to join "Uncle Karl" in disassociating those things from the life and teachings of Jesus we both considered to be the heart of the Gospel? Really, the answer is simple: Because I was absolutely convinced that the God behind that Gospel was not only real, but fully operational in my own life.

Armed with that conviction, I could make all kinds of excuses for God. Beginning with my friend Shonda's gang-rape in Camden and carrying all the way through to the devastating earthquake in Haiti in 2012, I took God off the hook by reminding myself that in order to make us capable of love, God had to give us free will, and that all human suffering flows—directly or indirectly—from our abuse of that freedom. Likewise, when even my most obviously legitimate prayers—for the healing of a child from cancer, for instance, or the deliverance of a woman from domestic abuse—went unanswered, I always imagined there must be a good reason God so seldom showed up. For as long as I believed in supernatural forces, God was not only real, but entirely blameless as well.

If any of this seems sarcastic or condescending, I don't mean it that way. The truth is I remember the certainty of my early days as a Christian with great fondness, and I'm still very much attracted to the idea of a good and loving God who understands all that we don't, speaks to us through the Bible, never fails to do right, and utterly triumphs over both sin and death in the end. Honestly, even now, if there was a magic pill that could enable me to truly believe all that again, once and for all time, I would gladly swallow it in a heartbeat, and not only because it would make my family so happy.

For better or worse, however, none of us really chooses what we believe. No matter how motivated we might be, our sense of what is real is beyond our control. Think about it, Christian friends: If a gun was put to your head, and you were absolutely convinced that unless you truly embraced Islam, you would be killed, along with your friends and family and ten thousand orphans who haven't yet trusted Jesus as their personal Lord and Savior, could you pull it off? Could you pass a polygraph test affirming you believe Muhammad actually split the moon in two and flew to heaven on a winged horse? For that matter, could you even will yourself to believe—as most people once did—that the Earth is the center of the universe, and all the stars revolve around it? No, you could not. Your mind is already made up about such things and, I would humbly submit, not entirely by you.

I'm not saying you can't be convinced of something new or different, of course, whether by evidence, argument, or personal experience. I'm just saying that, even when you very much want to, you don't get to decide what you think. All that convincing stuff, whether it comes from your parents or your preacher or a bunch of scientists, either persuades you or it doesn't. All you get to decide is what you do with what seems true to you.

Ever since my deconversion became well known, obviously sincere believers from all over the world have written, called, and visited, lovingly imploring me to reconsider. Sometimes they warn me of the eternal fires of hell, or lament that my enthusiasm for secular goodness might be leading others astray, but more often they ask me to seek God by fasting and praying, or they send long lists of Bible verses and books about Christian apologetics, perhaps forgetting that I spent most of my life as an evangelical urban missionary. While I very much appreciate their concerns, I often wonder why they hold me responsible for my obviously sincere lack of faith. After all, if Christianity is true, and there really is a God in heaven, he's the one to blame. As the apostle Paul puts it to the believers in Ephesus:

For by grace you have been saved through faith, and this is not your own doing; it is the gift of God—not the result of works, so that no one may boast. (Ephesians 2:8–9, NRSV)

That's right, according to Paul, none of us works our way into salvation, or even into the supernatural faith required to receive it. That faith is the gift of God, plain and simple. Which means, of course, that if there's anyone my dear Christian friends, those concerned folks who keep reaching out to me, and especially my still-believing parents ought to be imploring, it is God, not me.

In my many conversations with concerned Christians, I've been very clear on this point: I'd be mightily pleased to return to the fold, like a modern-day prodigal son, and to follow Jesus and sing of his love forever, if only I could believe again in the reality of God. I have an idea or two about the kind of evidence it would take to convince me, but honestly, I'm open to whatever the Holy Spirit sees fit to use. In the meantime, however, as with all of us, my faith is out of my hands. All I can do now is authentically respond to what seems to me the most important truth in the universe: Because there are no supernatural forces, this life is the only one we have.

You Reap What You Sow: How I See Bart's Deconversion

by Tony Campolo

WHENEVER I READ OR listen to Bart testify about his loss of faith, my first reaction is to blame myself. I know it doesn't make sense, especially because Bart was a middle-aged family man when he deconverted, but still I can't help it. Throughout my many years of ministry, I have spoken and corresponded with countless Christian parents whose adult children have rejected their Christianity in one way or another, and most of them feel the same way. As you can imagine, it was much easier for me to comfort and encourage such people when my own dear son was still following in my footsteps as a well-known evangelical leader. Now that he is a high-profile humanist instead, however, I must constantly remind myself that Bart's deconversion is primarily the result of his own decisions, not mine.

Of course, as he so eloquently expressed in his last chapter, Bart does not see it that way. Indeed, like so many secular humanists, he primarily attributes his deconversion to God's failure to "show up" and make Himself known. Not surprisingly, I dis-agree, both as a believer and as a social scientist. Permit me to explain.

As a university professor, I regularly taught a course called The Sociology of Religion, which always included Peter Berger and Thomas Luckmann's convincing cases that what individuals do and don't believe is highly contingent on what is affirmed to be reasonable by the individuals, groups, and institutions most important to them. According to Berger and Luckmann in their book, *The Social Construction of Reality* (1967), this phenomenon not only applies to the socialization of children but also and espe-cially to adults whose religious convictions strongly differ from the societies surrounding them. Indeed, Berger and Luckmann argue that the only way for an individual to maintain beliefs contrary to the dominant culture is to be a part of a close-knit, countercultural support group they call a "plausibility structure," wherein members meet regularly to reinforce and revitalize one another's beliefs and deconstruct all influences to the contrary. Within such a group, they point out, even convictions that might seem absurd to members of the dominant society remain com-pletely plausible, and in many cases virtually self-evident.

Any Christian who has spent a week at a church camp al-ready knows how a plausibility structure works. Such retreats perfectly illustrate how easy it is to create a powerful alterna-tive social reality that is diametrically opposed to the dominant culture. I vividly remember being driven out of the city and into the woods to a beautiful campground, where my church friends and I were greeted by attractive, enthusiastic counselors who immediately made us feel welcome. In short order we were reminded that no portable radios or televisions—today it might be laptops and cell phones—were permitted. In other words, all contact with the outside world was quickly cut off.

For the rest of the week, we enjoyed intensive interaction with other young people from very similar backgrounds. We ate and slept together, hiked and played together, and studied the Bible and prayed together. Every night our counselors gave inspirational talks about turning away from worldly pleasures for the greater joy of discipleship. Then, on the closing night of camp, there was always a campfire gathering. There, we'd sing seven or eight verses of "Kumbaya," and one of the leaders would call us campers to commit (or recommit) our lives to Christ. By that time, most of us were so caught up in that hyperspiritual mind-set that we didn't hesitate, knowing our peers would cheer us on as we stepped forward to dedicate (or rededicate) ourselves to following Jesus forever.

Many of those youthful decisions have lifelong effects. When talking to people in full-time Christian service, I often hear them say, "I made my decision to follow Jesus at camp." Of course, in order to last, such commitments must be repeated and reinforced, over and over again, especially in the context of a largely secular dominant culture. We ministers describe that process as follow-up and discipleship, but Berger and Luckmann would simply say we are providing vulnerable believers with a plausibility structure where continuing to believe in God, trust Jesus as Lord and Savior, and receive comfort and direction from the Holy Spirit is understood to be both right and entirely reasonable.

Not surprisingly, when I describe this sort of thing to my atheist and agnostic friends, they generally smile and say, "See! Your religious belief system is nothing more than a socially constructed reality," as though that alone discounts its validity.

What they fail to acknowledge, however, is that their secular belief system is socially constructed as well. For better or worse, what we human beings are able to believe about everything that matters—and especially about the reality of God—is largely determined by the most important individuals, groups, and institutions surrounding us.

At this point I want to be careful not to ascribe to plausibility structures the absolute power to determine what an individual does or does not believe. In fact, plausibility structures provide only the conditions wherein a particular belief system becomes and remains viable. Unfortunately, the secular society in which we live does not create a plausibility structure for the Gospel of Jesus Christ. That doesn't mean the Gospel isn't true, of course, but only that it is difficult if not impossible to hold on to that truth without regularly interacting with trusted friends and loved ones who recognize and affirm it.

After all, Christianity affirms a broad array of supernatural realities that would seem completely unreasonable to anyone whose understanding of truth is limited to what can be empirically proved and understood in purely rational terms. For example, I believe the same God who created the universe was later conceived by the Holy Spirit, born of a virgin as Jesus of Nazareth, and crucified to death to atone for the sins of humanity. I further believe He descended to hell, resurrected from the dead on the third day, and then ascended to heaven, and will one day return to undo every wrong in the world so that all His children can live with Him forever.

I know that to a secularist such beliefs seem ridiculous, but in the context of my Christian community, they are just the opposite. It is not that we don't recognize that the Gospel doesn't align with modern science. On the contrary, from the very beginning we have celebrated that fact. Biblical scholars have recently uncovered records indicating that members of the first-century church met every morning for spiritual renewal in order to resist being conformed to the dominant Roman-Hellenistic culture, and I for one am not surprised. As Paul wrote to the Christians in Corinth,

> *For the preaching of the cross is to them that perish foolishness; but unto us which are saved it is the power of God. For it is written, I will destroy the wisdom of the wise, and will bring to nothing the understanding of the prudent. Where is the wise? where is the scribe? where is the disputer of this world? hath not God made foolish the wisdom of this world? . . .*
>
> *Because the foolishness of God is wiser than men; and the weakness of God is stronger than men. For ye see your calling, brethren, how that not many wise men after the flesh, not many mighty, not many noble, are called: . . .*
>
> *But of him are ye in Christ Jesus, who of God is made unto us wisdom, and righteousness, and sanctification, and redemption: That, according as it is written, He that glorieth, let him glory in the Lord.*
> (1 Corinthians 1:18–20, 25–26, 30–31, KJV)

Clearly, Paul is saying that the Gospel has been set forth as impossible to understand in purely rational terms *on purpose*, so that nobody can mistake his or her salvation for anything other than a miraculous gift. In other words, the Gospel isn't supposed to be entirely logical or empirically provable. That's why we Christians need to keep reminding one another how it works— and how it has worked in our own lives—over and over again.

That's also why God has ordained for us the ultimate plausibility structure, otherwise known as the church of Jesus Christ.

I'm convinced that Bart was a committed Christian for many years largely because he remained deeply involved with a variety of fellowship groups, which combined to provide a plausibility structure that consistently contradicted the "wisdom" of our dominant American culture. Early on, all those youth groups, mission projects, and Bible studies—and the intimate friendships that grew out of them—enabled Bart to hold tightly to a set of beliefs that even our own scriptures acknowledge are "foolishness" to those living outside the faith community, in what secularists call "the real world." In the midst of such intense spiritual relationships and activities, he regularly experienced the presence of God in a visceral way, and every time that happened, the overall truth of the Christian narrative was once again confirmed. Later, when Bart became a full-time evangelical minister, he continued to be surrounded by people and institutions that enabled him to hold fast to the Gospel.

His story about nearly losing his faith in college is a good example. I well remember Bart's struggles with James Barr and his textual criticism, and the happiness we all felt when Bart found his way with the help of one of my own theological heroes, Karl Barth. What I also remember, however, is that Bart's study partner was also a deeply committed Christian, with whom he often prayed, along with Bart's girlfriend and the youth leader with whom he coached his church's junior high basketball team. Without such close fellowship, he might not have been so determined to work out his problems with the Bible. As it was, because he was still sure of God's presence, he kept looking until he found authentically Christian answers to his questions.

For many years, as I watched Bart wrestle with the same big issues that have troubled thoughtful believers since the dawn of time, I wasn't very worried that my beloved son would ultimately lose his faith. I knew Bart's theology would continue to change over time, and I understood that some of those changes might take him in a different direction from mine, but that didn't bother me. After all, I've wrestled with those big issues myself, and while I am surer than ever about some of the basics, my own theology is still very much a work in progress. On a daily basis, as I read my Bible and ask the Holy Spirit for guidance, I find that following Jesus keeps requiring me to change my mind. As one of my favorite bumper stickers says, "Be patient—God's not finished with me yet!"

As Bart and his family gradually stopped participating in a local congregation on a regular basis, however, I became deeply concerned. I understood his excuses, of course. By that time, he was traveling all over the country, speaking at conferences and on college campuses to raise money and recruit volunteers for his inner-city ministry. Besides being so busy, for a variety of reasons, Bart and his wife also had a hard time finding churches that were a good fit. Even so, Peggy and I desperately urged them to keep trying, especially after they had kids. Nevertheless, by the time they moved to Cincinnati to serve the poor more directly, the younger Campolos were essentially unchurched.

In Cincinnati, Bart and his wife, Marty, lived out the kind of sacrificial lifestyle to which I think Jesus calls us all. Eschewing a comfortable middle-class lifestyle, they relocated to a poverty-stricken neighborhood where they and their friends cared for some of America's most downtrodden people. One after another, they invited troubled young people to come live with their family, and spent countless hours securing housing for needy families. On a weekly basis, they fed dozens of their neighbors in a family-style setting. Despite doing such good works in the name of Jesus, and despite continuing to preach around the country, however, my son and his family became even more disconnected from church life. They still had many Christian friends, of course, but they participated in no regular fellowship.

To make matters worse, because so many of those he sought to serve were living self-defeating lifestyles marked by persistent violence, drug and alcohol abuse, dysfunctional family relationships, and dependency on government handouts, Bart soon began to openly assert that some people are incapable of being saved or transformed in any meaningful way. When this happened, I became even more alarmed.

Nikolay Berdyayev, the Russian existentialist philosopher, points out that when someone stops believing in the capacity of other people to grow and change and engage in noble and worthwhile pursuits, that individual eventually loses faith in God as well. Drawing on the epic novels of Fyodor Dostoyevsky, Berdyayev explains that to lose sight of the divine presence in even the lowliest person is the beginning of atheism. According to Berdyayev, the reverse is true as well—to lose faith in God is to lose faith in people. That's why the Great Commandment so closely ties together loving God with loving our neighbor; Jesus well knows we cannot do one without the other. As the apostle John puts it, *"For those who do not love a brother or sister whom they have seen, cannot love God whom they have not seen"* (1 John 4:20).

After reaching out to the seemingly hopeless men and women in his neighborhood, and seeing almost no positive results from his labors of love, Bart gave up on saving such people and decided his mission was merely to comfort them in their affliction instead. When my son no longer believed that literally anyone and everyone has possibilities for radical change, the seeds of doubt in his mind sprang up into full-grown agnosticism.

It is easy for me to sit in my affluent home and make this kind of judgment. I have never lived and worked in the trenches of urban ministry, nor did I ever have to endure the ministry disappointments Bart experienced year after year. Sometimes I wonder if my own faith would have held up as long as my son's had I been in his place. Nevertheless, albeit from my safe and secure vantage point, I continue to believe in miracles. More important, I have seen for myself the drastic and positive personal transformations accomplished through ministries like Teen Challenge, a Pentecostal drug rehabilitation ministry that reaches out to so-called throwaway people in cities around the world. Of course, in contrast to the latter versions of Bart's outreach, these folks rely on what they call "the infilling of the Holy Spirit" and practically never stop praying, fasting, singing hymns, and preaching the Gospel of Jesus Christ.

Indeed, another warning sign that Bart's faith was in trouble was his increasing tendency to avoid calling those to whom he preached into a personal relationship with Christ. He did a fine job of inviting young men and women to commit themselves to serving the poor and oppressed, but the idea of inviting the Holy Spirit to invade their hearts and minds seemed more and more distant from his messages.

While most of us assume that what we believe and think determines what we say and do, we preachers quickly learn that the reverse is just as true. In fact, what I declare from the pulpit has always had a huge impact on my worldview. Sociologists call this dialectic relationship between our words and actions "praxis," and in matters of faith, it is a powerful force. In my own life, I often find that no listener is more convinced or changed by what I say in my preaching than I am myself. Indeed, when asked why I am so committed to serving poor and oppressed people, the true answer is "Because that's what I'm always talking about." To rephrase the famous dictum of René Descartes, "I preach, therefore I am." So then, when Bart stopped emphasizing how only the death and resurrection of Jesus saves us from our sins, I knew it was only a matter of time before that same idea slipped out of his heart and mind as well.

While I am no nihilist, I tend to agree with Jean-Paul Sartre and Friedrich Nietzsche when it comes to human free will. In my opinion, who and what we become is ultimately the result of a long series of decisions that we make for ourselves. I think I am a Christian not only because God has chosen to love and save me but also because I have freely chosen to trust His Word and do His will. In opposition to secular social scientists who contend we human beings are biologically and socially determined in every way, I affirm our dignity as those who freely make the most important decisions that determine our nature and destiny.

In Bart's case, those important decisions included gradually distancing himself from the intense Christian fellowship that made his faith in God possible in the first place, giving up on the kinds of personal transformations that best demonstrate the power of the Holy Spirit, and ceasing to openly proclaim the Gospel of Jesus Christ. While I am very thankful that he didn't fall prey to other temptations that might have destroyed his family or undermined his character, I still hold him responsible for taking one fateful step after another away from God. To do otherwise would be to disrespect his independence as an adult or deny his dignity as a human being.

Oh, both my wife and I still ask ourselves where we went wrong and blame ourselves for saying too much or too little at certain points along the way. I worry that I should have set a better example by staying home and serving the poor myself instead of flying around the world talking about it, while Peggy wonders how different things might be had she already trusted Jesus when our kids were growing up. In the end, however, we keep reminding ourselves that Bart knew and loved God for more than thirty years, and that we did our best to support and encourage that relationship. And we keep praying, of course, on behalf of our prodigal son.

Ironically, it is Bart himself who has taught us how to pray for him. Secular as he is these days, his exegesis of Ephesians 2 is still right on the money. However we take care of it, our ability to believe—and therefore our ability to believe again—is always a gift from God. Therefore, rather than praying for Bart to soften his heart or change his mind or reopen his Bible or go back to church, I pray instead that the Holy Spirit will somehow dramatically overwhelm him the way Saul was overwhelmed on the road to Damascus, restoring his ability to look beyond the wisdom of the wise and see that the foolishness of God is ever so much wiser.

Life on the Other Side: The Happy Reality of Secular Humanism

by Bart Campolo

For the first few years after I lost my faith, I worked behind the scenes for a small international nonprofit, educating Americans about the Israeli-Palestinian conflict. I didn't advertise my emerging secular humanism, but I was open enough about my transition to draw out plenty of other post-Christians. While some were exhilarated by their newfound freedom, many more confessed to feeling lost and lonely outside the friendly confines of their former orthodoxy. When I asked those folks what they missed most, nobody ever mentioned the Ten Commandments, the Great Commission, or the notion that Jesus died for their sins, let alone arguing over marriage equality or worrying that their unbelieving loved ones might be bound for hell.

What those post-Christians really longed for, they told me, was everything else. They missed the music. They missed the hymn sings and potluck dinners. They missed meeting up with the same friends every week, to inspire and equip one another to live better lives. They missed raising their kids with other families that shared their values. They missed being able to find more like-minded people almost anywhere they moved. In other words, they missed the church.

Sometimes, if the people I talked with knew my background, they put me on the spot. "You were a minister, Bart," they pointed out. "You used to lead all that good stuff. Why don't you organize a church for people like us, who want to be good but don't believe in God?"

Look, everybody knows there are bunches of angry atheists running around out there, openly mocking the church and loudly proclaiming that organized religion poisons everything, but I will never be one of them. First of all, I have far too much love and gratitude for the many believers who have positively shaped my life to ever want to communicate disrespect for their communities and traditions. Second, and more importantly, I feel no disrespect. On the contrary, I think Christianity has been one of the greatest community-building forces in human history. I don't want to trash the church; I want to learn from it. I don't want to eliminate organized religion; I want to help develop a new and improved version of it—without the supernatural narrative—for people who genuinely want to be good without God.

Not coincidentally, *Good Without God* is the title of one of the most encouraging books I read immediately after I recovered from my bicycle crash. Written by Greg Epstein, the humanist chaplain at Harvard University, the book not only introduced me to the logic and language of secular humanism but also opened up the exciting possibility that I might get a second chance to be a vocational minister after all. The pastoral encounters with young people Greg described were almost identical to those I'd had myself back when I was running Mission Year, except for the fact that they revolved around two very different narratives offering two very different arguments for living a life of love. Reading about them, I realized that everything I'd learned about guiding people in that direction, both individually and as part of a movement, might be just as useful on the other side of faith. As a matter of fact, I'd barely finished the last page of the book before I tracked down Greg's number and telephoned him to ask if I could come see for myself the good work he was doing.

I'm not sure what I expected to find in Boston, but what shocked me there was not the difference between Greg's humanist chaplaincy and the countless Christian campus ministries I'd visited over the years, but rather the incredible similarity. The students I met were warm, friendly, and enthusiastic. The staff members were bright and articulate. The programming was a familiar blend of inspirational meetings and lectures, small group discussions, outreach, social events, and service projects. It wasn't big or fancy, but it felt like home.

What I didn't find, of course, was any talk of God or faith. Instead, the conversations I overheard were about everything from cognitive science, vegetarianism, and TED talks to racial politics, an upcoming LGBTQ solidarity march, and coming out as secular to your family. Nevertheless, the overall atmosphere at Harvard's Humanist Hub felt exactly like every good youth group I've ever known. And Greg Epstein? Well, Greg was and is a lot like me. We're both bald, we both love to talk, and we're both natural-born community builders. Looking at his work, I saw my future.

In the summer of 2014, at Greg's suggestion, I reached out to Dr. Varun Soni, the dean of Religious Life at the University of Southern California, to see what he thought of my idea of building missional communities for people who don't believe in God. Before I knew it, he was recruiting me. Dr. Soni explained that USC didn't define religion in terms of specific belief systems but rather as the quest to answer life's ultimate questions: What is the nature of the universe? Where do we come from and what happens when we die? Who defines good and evil? How can we make the most of our lives? There were more than forty religious directors on campus, Dr. Soni told me, representing a wide variety of supernatural religions, but there was nobody addressing the communal needs of USC's rapidly growing secular population. I would have to raise my own funds, he cautioned, but becoming the first humanist chaplain at USC was a great opportunity to organize the kind of congregation I had in mind. A few weeks later, Marty and I were on our way to Los Angeles.

What do I do at USC? Practically speaking, I do the same things you would expect any university chaplain to do. I show up at campus events, speak in classes and dorm meetings, host community gatherings, sponsor a student fellowship, offer pastoral care and comfort when tragedy strikes, and meet one-on-one with loads of students and professors to encourage and support their spiritual growth.

If that last phrase seems strange to you, it shouldn't. Just because someone doesn't believe in God doesn't mean they aren't interested in having transcendent experiences, cultivating compassion, expressing gratitude, and making meaning through loving relationships and sacrificial service. Indeed, recent demographic studies suggest that while fewer young adults are identifying with traditional religions, there is an increasing hunger for what social commentators have begun to call secular spirituality. Those hungry ones are my target audience, both here at USC and as I speak, write, and podcast around the world, and my message to them is simple: If you want to fully actualize your noblest values, you've got to find like-minded people and band together. Nobody becomes or remains good in isolation. We have to help one another grow.

I'm not talking about organizing more old-school atheist clubs that get together to rail against traditional religion, obsess over the separation of church and state, and congratulate one another for being so rational, either. If those people were *really* rational, I often think, they would pay more attention to data that clearly indicates such negative approaches are doomed to fail at making things better. There's only ever been one way to build that kind of movement: First you have to teach your friends to love one another, and then you have to teach them how to attract and include outsiders by loving them as well. That's why my new ideal ministry is practically identical to my old one, except that these days I rely on reason, science, and common sense to convince people that love is the most excellent way.

For example, on any given Sunday evening, Marty and I invite thirty or forty students to join us for a big, family-style dinner, partly because young people flock to food, and partly because there's loads of evidence that eating together lowers people's stress levels and heightens their sense of connectivity. Alcohol at a frat party does the same thing, of course, but loosening up that way doesn't accelerate the kinds of meaningful conversations and relationships I'm trying to foster. Instead, I usually put index cards with a few leading questions on each table and make sure that our friendliest, most empathetic group members spread out and pay special attention to those who aren't as socially adept. Then, in between dinner and dessert, I deliver a short talk about making the most of this life, and, after the dishes have been cleared, I lead the group in one of those goofy games I learned at summer camp. The "sermon" is important for communicating our group's collective values and common language, but what matters most is that my leaders, Marty, and I work together to create a warm and welcoming atmosphere that draws people back often enough that we can actually get to know and care about one another.

Frankly, recruiting new members to a humanist community and getting people interested in and excited about adopting a humanist identity is much easier for me than Christian evangelism ever was. Back then, even if I managed to convince someone that my friends and I were a good and loving group, there inevitably came that moment when the newcomer realized that joining us required a fairly colossal leap of faith. To be a card-carrying member of the secular community at USC, however, you don't have to believe anything for which you don't have clear and compelling evidence. All you have to do is genuinely want to be a better person.

At some point each week, I simply walk across campus, looking for someone who wants to strike up a conversation. Often I'll just sit down in the student union and ask the students around me what they study and why, and how they feel about what they're learning. They politely brush me off sometimes, but usually they're happy to talk, and invariably they ask what I do at USC. When I tell them I'm the humanist chaplain, they generally reply, "What does that mean?" When I tell them it means

I'm here to nurture and support anyone who wants to become a truly good person and make the world a better place, but doesn't believe in God, they almost invariably light up. "Hey, that's me! Tell me more about your group. How do I join?" It's not hard to get people interested when your community is all about values instead of beliefs.

Of course, I run into plenty of believers on campus as well. Sometimes they want to debate me, but more often they seem happy to know a group like ours exists, especially once they realize I'm not interested in undermining anyone else's faith. In fact, most of the Christian students I meet identify with at least some part of my story, even though they've come to different conclusions. Mainly, however, I just listen to them talk about their journeys. When believers are happily growing, I encourage them to keep doing what they're doing, especially if their family and friends are believers as well. After all, my goal isn't to destroy Christianity; my goal is to help as many people as possible commit themselves to loving relationships, meaningful work, and an ever-deepening sense of wonder and gratitude. If supernatural faith is still helping someone in that direction, I step back and celebrate. Depending on the conversation, I'm sometimes even able to steer a believer to helpful resources in his or her own tradition.

My great enemies aren't sincere supernatural believers and their traditions, but rather the darker forces that threaten to undermine human flourishing: greed, violence, ignorance, intolerance, hunger, loneliness, boredom. That's why getting USC students to self-identify as secular humanists and join our fellowship isn't the end goal of my work here, but only the beginning. For me, secular ministry is mainly about getting nonbelievers to fully commit their lives to . . . well, to life itself.

While reading Greg Epstein's book was the beginning of my humanist ministry, it wasn't until I read Ursula Goodenough's devotional classic, *The Sacred Depths of Nature* (1998), that I found the words to express that ministry's ultimate goals. Goodenough is a biologist and, like me, the child of a Protestant minister who understands that whether or not people believe in God, everybody needs some kind of religion. She describes it this way:

> *In the end, each of these religions addresses two fundamental human concerns: How Things Are and Which Things Matter. How Things Are becomes formulated as a Cosmology or Cosmos: How the universe came to be, how humans came to be, what happens after we die, the origins of evil and tragedy and natural disaster. Which Things Matter becomes codified as a Morality or Ethos: the Judaic Ten Commandments, the Christian Sermon on the Mount, the Five Pillars of Islam, the Buddhist Vinaya, the Confucian Five Relations. The role of religion is to integrate the Cosmology and the Morality, to render the cosmological narrative so rich and compelling that it elicits our allegiance and our commitment to its emergent moral understandings. As each culture evolves, a unique Cosmos and Ethos appear in its co-evolving religion. For billions of us, back to the first humans, the stories, ceremonies, and art associated with our religions-of-origin are central to our matrix.*

As Goodenough sees it, because population growth, unfettered corporate power, increasing economic instability, ethnic and political conflict, rampant environmental degradation, and above all climate change are global threats to human welfare, the time has come for us to develop a globally shared religion that somehow transcends our various cultural traditions without seeking to overthrow them.

From her perspective, the first part of that project—a globally shared Cosmos—ought to be easy. As she says,

> *How things are is, well,* how things are: *our scientific account of Nature, an account that can be called The Epic of Evolution. The Big Bang, the formation of stars and planets, the origin and evolution of life on this planet, the advent of human consciousness and the resultant evolution of cultures—this is the story, the one story, that has the potential to unite us, because it happens to be true.*

In order to realize that potential, however, that Cosmos must be expressed in warm, resonant ways that generate a genuinely religious response. In other words, we need to learn to talk about our scientific understanding of nature—and especially our part in it—so clearly, so beautifully, and so passionately that, as Goodenough puts it, "we all experience a solemn gratitude that we exist at all, share a reverence for how life works, and acknowledge a deep and complex imperative that life continue."

This is where I think the secular movement has not yet stepped up to the plate. We have the best, most majestic, most miraculously unlikely and yet easy-to-believe narrative the world has ever known, but with a few notable exceptions, we haven't yet learned how to make it sing, let alone how to preach it. If you don't believe me, just take a look around. More and more people are losing faith in any kind of supernaturalism, but very few of them are becoming fully enthusiastic, genuinely religious naturalists.

As I always tell my students, if this life really is all we have, the only rational choice is to make the most of it by proactively building loving relationships, doing work that makes things better for other people, and cultivating a sense of gratitude for the wonders of the universe and the privilege of being alive and conscious in the first place. That commitment isn't a leftover from my Christian days, but rather a heartfelt response to my new understanding of the incredibly improbable way that I came to exist and what will—or at least what could—happen after I die. I am not just a student of nature and history after all; I am part of them. I love this Walt Whitman poem:

> O me! O life! of the questions of these recurring,
> Of the endless trains of the faithless, of cities fill'd with the foolish,
> Of myself forever reproaching myself, (for who more foolish than I, and
>   who more faithless?)
> Of eyes that vainly crave the light, of the objects mean, of the struggle
>   ever renew'd,
> Of the poor results of all, of the plodding and sordid crowds I see
>   around me,
> Of the empty and useless years of the rest, with the rest me
>   intertwined,
> The question, O me! so sad, recurring—What good amid these,
>   O me, O life?
>
>   Answer.
> That you are here—that life exists and identity,
> That the powerful play goes on, and you may contribute a verse.
>
>   —"Oh me! Oh life!," Leaves of Grass (1905)

To be a secular humanist is to embrace that opportunity and to dedicate yourself to making your verse a truly good one, not because you will be rewarded for it after you die, but for the pure joy of imagining people yet to be born enjoying a world you helped make possible for them, whether they know it or not.

As teenagers, my closest friends and I were inspired by Dietrich Bonhoeffer's Christian classic *The Cost of Discipleship* (1937), because it made following Jesus seem like such a bold, radical choice. Like so many young people, we weren't looking for a safe, comfortable lifestyle, but rather a revolutionary movement worthy of our total commitment. When Bonhoeffer contrasted the "cheap grace" of the establishment with the "costly grace" of true discipleship, we immediately knew which one we wanted. My buddies and I weren't interested in the stale trappings of dogmatic religion, but only in a dynamic, personal relationship with the living Christ and all the heroic adventure that came with it. In the name of Jesus, our mission was to save the world.

Everyone in our group didn't feel that way, of course, and even my friends and I waxed and waned in our devotion, but there is no question that our powerful sense of collective mission held us together and inspired us to sacrifice for the cause. Our prayer meetings, Bible studies, evangelistic retreats, and mission trips weren't just for fun; we were building a movement, and in the process, each of us was constantly shoring up his or her own commitment to our shared values. The rest of the church was stuck in the mud, we thought, but we true believers would show them the way.

That's exactly how I want my students to feel about their own role in history, in part because it positively transforms their lives in the present, but also because I believe the fate of humanity depends on their willingness to make profound sacrifices for the sake of future generations, and on their ability to inspire others to do the same. No one is coming to save us, after all. Peace and justice are things we human beings carve out of chaos. Civilization is not and cannot be taken for granted. If we do not solve our many problems, they will overtake and destroy us, and the key that unlocks all of them is learning to love one another. In other words, the bad news and the good news of not believing in God are one and the same: The only hope and meaning in the universe are those which we make for ourselves, and in order to survive we must always make more.

Of course, the radical, "let's save the world" way of life I want my students to embrace for themselves and share with others is practically as simple as the one I shared with my high school friends. I want them to read books and listen to podcasts that excite their imaginations, and swap them back and forth with one another. I want them to get angry about injustices and plot new ways to fight them. I want them to be on the lookout for people who are lost or lonely and work together to include them. I want them to write anthems of awe and wonder at the majesty of nature, and liturgies that call us to respond accordingly. I want them to stay up late at night, falling in love with big ideas and pushing one another to keep doing the stuff that really matters, the way the best young people in every religion always have. Because, strange as it sounds to say it, secular humanism is indeed my religion.

To use my father's language, secular humanism can and should operate as a global plausibility structure much like the Christian church, albeit with reason standing in for faith, and science in the place of supposedly divine guidance. Recalling his quotations from 1 Corinthians 1, we must apply *"the wisdom of the world"* even as our believing brethren apply *"the foolishness of God"* by building countless local communities that inspire and equip us to be and do our best. When that happens, I am quite certain believers and secularists alike will be pleasantly surprised by how little we differ in living out our most cherished values, and by how many of those values we hold in common.

THE HEART OF THE MATTER:
WHY HUMANISM DOESN'T
WORK WITHOUT JESUS

by Tony Campolo

As UNHAPPY AS I am about my son's departure from Christianity, I am proud of his ongoing commitment to building transformational communities, and gratified by the obvious similarities between what he learned about ministry from me and my evangelical friends and what he teaches his students at the University of Southern California. I am also relieved, of course, having encountered many former Christians who are openly hostile to any kind of organized spirituality and who communicate nothing but contempt for the believing friends and family members they have left behind. For the parents of such angry atheists, I have nothing but compassion.

For the Christian parents of positive secular humanists like Bart, however, I have some advice: Take every opportunity to affirm and encourage your children whenever they say or do something that reflects your Kingdom values, and let them know that you see a direct connection between their behavior and the love of God, even if they don't. Doing so demonstrates that you notice and appreciate your kids' goodness while maintaining your own understanding of its ultimate source, and also opens up opportunities for you to talk about what gets lost when God drops out of the picture.

In the case of Bart's humanist chaplaincy, it seems to me that the most important thing that is missing is an eternal, unshakable foundation for the lifestyle he's selling to his students. In simple terms, I think he needs Jesus. Allow me to explain.

As I mentioned earlier, in the midsixties I was unexpectedly given the chance to teach sociology to Ivy Leaguers at the University of Pennsylvania. In lectures and seminars, I was confronted time and again by bright and serious students who would not allow me the luxury of dealing with my questions, but instead demanded that we discuss theirs. Most of all, these secular young people wanted to know what it means to be human and how humanness can be achieved. All their other questions were related to this dominant one. Their cries for social justice expressed their hope for a world where everyone was free to self-actualize. Their interest in psychology centered on reaching their fullest potential. Even their experimentation with psychedelic drugs revealed their desire to heighten awareness so that life could be appreciated and enjoyed in greater depth.

In the ferment of that setting, I had to rework what I believed in order to give Christian answers to the questions that burned in the hearts and minds of my students. Much to my surprise, some of them were converted to the Christian faith, and it was not long before members of my department began to grumble that I had turned my courses into evangelistic church services. Looking back, I must confess that they were probably right. However, the fact that students listened with intense interest to what the Bible has to say convinced me that we don't need to be ashamed of the Gospel of Christ. One day, when I asked my senior seminar students what they wanted out of life, the class came alive.

"I want to become human—fully human," one of my students blurted out. He stood up, which was unusual behavior in the informal setting of the seminar room. "We all want to be human," he said. "We don't know how to become human, and nothing that I've heard in this class up to this point has provided any hints."

"What do you mean by 'human'?" I inquired. "Can you describe the traits of humanness? Can you list the characteristics of humanness? Can you give me some idea of what it is you want to achieve? After all, how can I tell you how to become human when you have not told me what that means?"

"Come off it," he said. "Everybody knows what it means to be human! It means to be loving, infinitely loving; sensitive, perfectly sensitive; aware, totally aware; empathetic, completely empathetic; forgiving, endlessly forgiving. I could go on, but I would only be elaborating on the obvious. Everyone here knows what I am talking about when I say 'humanness,' and you do too, so stop putting me on."

"Okay," I said. "I was putting you on. I do know what you mean by humanness. But I must probe a bit further. You know something of love, something of empathy, and something of forgiveness. Even if you possess these traits to a very limited degree, you obtained them somehow. Were you born with them? Were they part of your biological makeup? The limited humanity in your personhood—where did it come from? What was its source?"

"You're putting me on again!" he shouted angrily. "This is a sociology class and you're a sociologist. You know that whatever qualities of humanness I possess were obtained by the process of socialization. If I am forgiving, it is because I associated with forgiving people and took on their traits and likeness. If I possess a sense of awareness to life, it is only because I interacted with people who lived this way. You know all that, so what are you trying to do?"

"What I am trying to do," I responded, "is to drive you back to a simple definition of socialization you learned in the introductory course. Remember how the textbook said, 'Socialization is the process whereby *Homo sapiens* become human'? Do you remember, we explained to you that if at the moment of birth you were separated from all human beings and raised by wolves in a forest, twenty years later you would possess none of those traits that you have so eloquently suggested are evidence of humanness?

"Without human interaction you would have no language with which to think. You would have no categories with which to interpret reality. All the human traits that you listed would be lacking. You would not even have a consciousness of self, for without social relationships you would never develop the reflective capacities that are essential for self-awareness. It is only by adopting the perspective of a significant other that you become conscious that you are an existing person. In short, without interaction with other human beings, you would have the form of a man, but none of the traits. Your humanity is a gift of society. You become what the people who socialize you are."

"What are you trying to prove?" he asked. "Are you telling me that society makes me human? I feel just the opposite. I feel that society is dehumanizing me. It leaves me feeling alienated and unloved. It reduces me to a thing; it doesn't make me into a person."

I was setting him up for the proclamation of the Gospel. "Look," I said, "what I'm trying to tell you is that the traits of humanness are gained only by interacting with those who possess them. If you have an intimate and sustained relationship with somebody who is very loving, you will become loving too. You know this from your own experience. Haven't you ever been with someone who was so human that when your time with that person was over, you felt your humanity had been enhanced, enlivened, and raised to a higher level? What I am trying to explain is that you will become only as human as the person who becomes the significant other in your life, the one to whom you relate most intimately."

"That's terrible!" he responded. "You're telling me that if I want to be fully human, if I want to be the totally actualized person that Abraham Maslow asks me to be, if I want to become everything I have the potential to be, then I need to have a relationship with somebody who is all of those things already. But don't you understand? I don't know anybody like that. What's more, I doubt if there is anybody like that. If you're right, I can never become fully human, because there's no one I can relate to who has achieved this heightened state of being."

It was the perfect setup and I think he knew it. I believe he anticipated what I was about to say.

"Yes, there is," I responded. "His name is Jesus. Read the New Testament. Read it honestly and openly. Read the four Gospels specifically. Learn about Jesus, and, as you learn about Him, ask a very simple question: Doesn't Jesus possess the fullness of humanity? Isn't He infinitely loving, endlessly forgiving, totally empathetic, and completely aware of people in the world in which He lives?

"You might ask how someone who lived two thousand years ago can answer your need for a humanizing relationship here and now. But you know my answer. You know that I am convinced that the Jesus described in the New Testament is resurrected from the grave, is present here and now, and invites you into the kind of relationship that holds your only hope for becoming what He is. You will probably say that the bad news is that He doesn't really exist, but I am trying to declare the good news that He really does. He wants to be personally related to you and He wants you to allow Him to transform you into His likeness."

Surprisingly, he and my other students were fascinated. They had all heard about the Jesus who died on the cross to save them from hell. From televangelists they had learned that if you believe in Jesus, you might get rich or be healed from cancer. But they had never before heard about a Jesus who humanizes. When the class hour came to an end, my students didn't want to stop. One of them invited everyone back to his apartment so we could keep the discussion going, and, after a quick call home to excuse myself from dinner, I joined the others there.

"Look," I resumed, "as I was listening to you list the traits of humanness, something kept telling me that you were also describing what God is like. God is all the things that you are telling me you want to be. Then it hit me—humanness and Godness are one and the same. You want to be conformed to the image of God—you want to be everything that Jesus was and is. What you call being human is really being Christlike."

At first that thought seemed blasphemous, but before I could dismiss it, a host of Bible verses flowed into my consciousness. In John 1:12, we are told that if we have a relationship with Jesus Christ, we will become *"children of God."* And the same thing is written by the apostle Paul, in Romans 8:15–17 (KJV):

> *For ye have not received the spirit of bondage again to fear; but ye have received the Spirit of adoption, whereby we cry, Abba, Father. The Spirit itself beareth witness with our spirit, that we are the children of God: And if children, then heirs; heirs of God, and joint-heirs with Christ; if so be that we suffer with him, that we may be also glorified together.*

Paul seems to be telling us that through Jesus we can become like Jesus, addressing God as "Abba" (equivalent to our word "Daddy") and possessing all the traits and qualities that my students called human.

One of my students said, "If Godness is humanness and vice versa, then we need a new way of talking about Jesus. Jesus is God *because* He is fully human, not in spite of His humanness. When I was a kid growing up in Sunday school, it seemed weird to me that God could be a man, but if I follow what you are saying, it is the most logical thing in the world. Jesus was God because He was fully human and He is fully human *because* He was God. In Jesus, everything that God *is* was revealed and everything that a human being is supposed to be was realized, and both of these were one and the same. Jesus was not God in spite of the fact that He was human; He was God *because* He was human; and He was and is the only fully human being that ever lived."

"That's right," I chimed in. "Each of the rest of us is still in the process of becoming human. Only Jesus is the fullness of what we aspire to become. When we become like Jesus, we do not become pious persons with holier-than-thou dispositions. Instead, we become people who manifest the 'fruits of the Spirit,' which in reality are the qualities of humanness. The Bible says: *'By contrast the fruit of the Spirit is love, joy, peace, patience, kindness, generosity, faithfulness, gentleness, and self-control . . .'* [Galatians 5:22–23, NASB]."

My young friend was now enthusiastically involved in the discussion, working intensely to spell out more of the implications of our developing theology: "What we are dealing with here leads us to an understanding of goodness and evil that is very different from what I've been taught. I was made to believe that a person is good when he obeys the set of rules that God has dictated in the Bible, and that a person is evil when he disobeys those laws. Now we are talking about goodness as anything that enhances the humanity of the individual, and evil as anything that diminishes it. For instance, the evil of hating somebody is that it diminishes my humanity, which is another way of saying that it makes me less like Jesus. On the other hand, good is doing something that helps someone else become more human and, in the process, becoming more human myself."

"You are really onto something!" I shot back. Suddenly I felt like a student myself. "Your formulation makes it clear that sin is tied up in social interaction. You are reminding me that I cannot realize my higher potentialities of humanness without engaging in the kind of activities that humanize other people, and that the dehumanization of other people causes me to lose the image of God. If we follow that line of thinking, then something like racism is wrong because it leads to treating some people as less than human and, hence, diminishes the humanity of both the victim and the practitioner.

"You're also helping me rethink sex. I've always figured that the sins of the flesh were desires and practices of sexuality outside of marriage. I assumed that sex was good so long as you did 'it' with the right person, following the rules of the church, and evil only if you failed to meet those requirements. Now I see that even the sexual act between a husband and wife is evil if it leaves either partner feeling degraded or objectified instead of loved."

Based on this realization, I made a simple statement: "To be saved from sin is to be delivered from this and every other kind of alienation. It is to enter into a personal relationship with the ultimate human, being transformed into His likeness to enjoy the ecstasy of full aliveness."

"Then I want to be saved," my student said. "If salvation means becoming fully human, then I want it. The religion upon which I was raised conveyed the idea that being saved was being delivered from the punishment of an angry God. I was made to believe that He is out to get anybody who does not agree with the Apostles' Creed. I thought if I believed all the right things and said 'yes' to all the right questions, I would go to heaven. And if I didn't, I would go to hell. I was taught that God would burn anybody who didn't believe that He loved them. Now you're telling me that being saved isn't about heaven or hell. It's about becoming human here and now. It's about entering into a process whereby my potentialities for humanness are actualized."

"I didn't say there is no afterlife," I responded. "As a matter of fact, the afterlife is an essential part of my belief about humanization. I believe that the process of being fully humanized cannot be completed during the course of our respective lifetimes. However, we can live in the hope that we will become fully human when we are fully united with Jesus after death. Becoming fully human is what heaven is all about."

"All of this sounds good to me," he answered, "but there's one gigantic problem left. I need you to explain to me how it is possible to establish a personal relationship with this Jesus who incarnates humanness. Please don't tell me that I just need to say a little prayer inviting Jesus into my heart. Explain to me in terms that make sense how I can meet this resurrected Jesus of yours, who will enable me to overcome the feeling of alienation that plagues my existence."

I sat back in the overstuffed maroon sofa that was the main piece of furniture in this typical student apartment. The eyes of Che Guevara stared down at me from the poster on the wall. Che seemed to be asking the question too. All the students eagerly leaned forward. Everything hung on my answer.

"Jesus can be found exactly where He said," I told them. "He told us that He did not dwell in temples and churches that we build in His honor. Instead, He encouraged us to look for Him in one another. He said, 'You are my temples; I dwell in you.' What I am trying to say is that the Jesus who incarnated God two thousand years ago is mystically present and waiting to be discovered in every person you and I encounter. I am claiming that every one of us is a priest who can communicate Jesus to those whom we meet, and that those whom we meet are priests who can communicate Jesus to each of us. Consider the very obvious fact that all of us are aware that there is something sacred in every other person. Something about each of them makes us believe that each is of infinite value and worth. Usually we do not bother to name this sacred presence we encounter in others, but we know it is real and that it requires respect.

"According to Martin Buber, there is, in addition to those traits of another person that can be known objectively and described verbally, a quality of being that is transcendental. He refers to this sacred quality of the other person as 'Thou.' Buber believes that if 'I' (that transcendental dimension of my self-hood) surrender to an intimate oneness with 'Thou,' alienation and estrangement will be overcome and humanness will be experienced. Buber calls such a relationship 'I-Thou.'"

I continued, "Such encounters are not normative in the everyday relationships we have with each other. Usually we have what Buber calls 'I-It' relationships, wherein the other person is nothing more than a thing or an object. He or she is a student, a worker, a Democrat, or a Presbyterian. In 'I-It' relationships, the other person is not encountered with reverence, but rather is reduced to a typical representative of a class of creatures who perform a particular function. The man who collects my fare on the bus is simply a bus driver. The woman who handles my legal affairs is only a lawyer. Such persons are no more than the roles they play. I confront them as though they were objects. I may try to be just and kind to them, and on a good day we may smile at each other politely, but our relationships go no deeper.

"On the other hand, 'I-Thou' relationships offer me far more. In such an encounter, each person surrenders to the other, and the two of us become one. Only later do I recognize that that precious and wonderful experience has become part of me.

Only later do I understand it as a sublime moment in which 'I' have temporarily felt the ecstatic joys of full humanity.

"Buber goes on to suggest that in every 'I-Thou' encounter, God is present not as an object or a concept that can be apprehended as an 'It,' but rather as Yahweh, 'the Eternal Thou,' who can be known only in the sacredness of the other person. So then, the resurrected Jesus can be met only in fellowship. That is why He says in scripture, *'where two or three are gathered together in my name, there am I in the midst of them'* [Matthew 18:20, KJV]. That is why the Bible tells us that any man who says he loves God but hates his brother is a liar, for it is only in loving others that we can experience God.

"I believe many people have experienced the humanizing power of Jesus through 'I-Thou' relationships without being aware of what was really going on. They encountered Jesus and were transformed by His love, and yet they didn't know who He was. Jesus is our only savior, but not everybody who is being saved recognizes that fact. Indeed, the Bible promises that there will be many surprises on Judgment Day. Some who claimed to know Jesus will be turned away because they ignored the needs of other people, while others who thought they had no relationship with Him will be welcomed into His Kingdom. He will explain that whenever they fed the hungry, clothed the naked, or ministered to the sick and lonely, He was right there. Jesus wasn't just talking symbolically when He said, *'Inasmuch as ye have done it unto one of the least of these my brethren, ye have done it unto me'* [Matthew 25:40, KJV]."

After I finished, there was a long silence. "I can't buy it," one of the students said. "Neither can I," said another. Finally, the student who had carried most of the conversation looked me in the eye. "I'm not sold yet, either," he said, "but I'll think about it."

After we parted ways that day, I prayed for those students in much the same way I pray for Bart now. First I thanked God for giving them such a deep desire for moral goodness, and then I asked God to help them see that without Jesus that hunger can never be fully satisfied.

Something else I wanted my students to recognize is that with secularism there isn't much of a moral imperative. If there is no God, then anything is permissible, says Dmitri in Fyodor Dostoyevsky's classic novel *The Brothers Karamazov*. Like me, Dmitri sees that in a world without a clear, permanent, objective moral foundation, right and wrong are entirely subjective categories, open to redefinition by any society or individual as it, he, or she sees fit. As much as Bart and his fellow secular humanists talk about pursuing goodness, they have no common, definitive example of the goodness they are talking about, and no way to access the spiritual resources necessary to follow that example. They are adrift, I think, whether or not they know it. Perhaps the madman of Nietzsche's parable ("Parable of the Madman," 1882) puts it best, as he rants about the "death" of God:

> *Whither are we moving now? Away from all suns? Are we not perpetually falling? Backward, sideward, forward, in all directions? Is there any up or down left? Are we not straying as through an infinite nothing? Do we not feel the breath of empty space? Has it not become colder? Is it not more and more night coming on all the time?*

Simplistic as it sounds, there is no better antidote for that coldness, and no more reliable moral guide than the question originally posed by Charles Sheldon in the novel *In His Steps* (1896): What would Jesus do? While God's will is certainly echoed and reflected in other cultures and religions around the world, and in the universally available wisdom that theologians call natural revelation, I believe it finds its fullest expression in the life and teachings of Jesus. Furthermore, I believe only Christ can enable each of us to fully actualize our human potential.

THE DARK SIDE OF GRACE: WHY JESUS DOESN'T WORK FOR ME

by Bart Campolo

My FATHER'S ACCOUNT OF his conversation with those UPenn students reminds me that such immediacy was always the evangelical gold standard for Christian discipleship. Every time another testimony, praise song, or devotional book described intimacy with Jesus, I felt my lack of it so much that it hurt. Listening to the hymn "I Come to the Garden Alone," I ached for Jesus to walk with me and talk with me and tell me I was his own. I believed he was real, but much to my chagrin, Jesus certainly wasn't my best friend.

Occasionally I was honest about my frustration, but more often I described the relationship I wanted with Jesus as if I already had it to cover my embarrassment in the midst of fellow believers. It wasn't until the latter part of my Christian journey that I realized how many of us were like the townspeople in Hans Christian Andersen's story *The Emperor's New Clothes,* fearfully pretending—and sometimes even convincing ourselves—we were seeing what our peers were so excited about, only to discover that everyone else was doing the same thing.

I spent many years hearing and preaching about the critical importance of an intimate, personal relationship with Jesus, but I never fully understood what those words meant. *How could I possibly have a personal relationship with someone who lived and died more than two thousand years ago?* I wondered. Even if I granted that Jesus rose from the dead and ascended into heaven, the right hand of God seemed much too far away for us to really get to know each other. *Besides,* I thought, *wasn't it the Holy Spirit that I was supposed to be relating to on a daily basis?*

Trust me, I'm not kidding here. In all the time I was a Christian—including my four years as a religious studies major at Haverford College and Brown University—I never figured out the salient difference between the resurrected Jesus and the Holy Spirit. Try as I might, the doctrine of the Trinity always eluded me, on both a theological and practical level. Even during those transcendent moments when I felt certain I heard the voice of God, I was never quite sure which member of the Godhead was doing the talking.

What I did know, however, was that my father and the rest of the evangelical community almost always describe their faith in terms of Jesus. To them, Jesus is and always has been God's ultimate expression, and his red-lettered words are the keys that unlock the true meaning of the Bible. Jesus is Lord and Savior. Jesus is the way, the truth, and the life. Jesus is the answer. In a very real sense, when it comes to that kind of Christianity, knowing Jesus in a personal way is the whole ball of wax.

To me, however, Jesus is almost entirely inaccessible. I've never seen his photograph, listened to a recording of his voice, or read a single sentence that can be surely ascribed to him, let alone met him in person or known someone else who did. Like the rest of the world, all I have to go on are four brief, highly redacted, obviously biased accounts of his life and times, which even in their original form were written some decades after his death, and aren't entirely consistent with one another. I know plenty of folks who claim those accounts clearly reveal his personality, but as far as I'm concerned, the biblical record of Jesus is far too sketchy for anyone to claim they really know Jesus's character.

Among the many important things I don't know about Jesus: whether he was a good carpenter; how he felt about Joseph not being his real father; his sexual orientation; his perspectives on slavery, abortion, and just war; his favorite kind of anything; his sense of humor; his best friend; why he raised Lazarus from the dead but nobody else; what he thought about between the crucifixion and the resurrection; and why he didn't make sure at least one of his disciples took better notes. I mean, seriously, I know way more about Abraham Lincoln—or Michael Jackson for that matter—than I do about Jesus.

In any case, the whole idea of having an intimate, personal relationship with a spiritual being strikes me as highly unrealistic. Such relationships are hard enough for us human beings to form with one another, after all. "What Would Jesus Do?" asked a million plastic bracelets, but I still have no idea. For goodness' sake, I don't know what my wife would do half the time, and we've been intimately acquainted for thirty years!

As a Christian, I answered such complaints by appealing to divine inspiration. We cannot truly understand or interpret the scriptural accounts of Jesus, I used to remind people, unless and until we are guided by the Holy Spirit. Given our limited and fallible human minds, we can know the truth only if God super-naturally invades our consciousness and reveals it.

Now I think what I experienced as a supernatural outside force was actually just the natural inner workings of my own brain. There's lots of evidence to support that conclusion, of course, but what originally led me to it wasn't psychology and neuroscience, but rather this simple observation: Despite the divine guidance of the Holy Spirit and more than two thousand years to work out the kinks, every Christian church and individual believer sees Jesus differently than all the rest, and each one of them is convinced that, thanks be to God, their vision is the fairest of them all.

Of course, those various visions reveal more about the values of the people who hold them than they do about Jesus himself. I may have only a faint idea of who the historical Jesus really was or what he cared about, but by reading or listening to any given Christian describe him, I can learn a great deal about who that person really is and what he or she cares about.

Not surprisingly, I very much like my father's Jesus, not only for his great compassion but also for his longtime commitment to social justice, environmental responsibility, and women's rights, not to mention his more recent embrace of marriage equality. I'm just kidding about that last part, of course, because everyone knows it isn't Jesus who finally changed his mind about our LGBTQ friends, but rather my father who changed his mind about Jesus.

I did the same thing as a Christian. Over and over again, I adjusted my vision of Jesus to reflect my latest values and understanding of the world. The good news was that the Lord I ended up with was quite literally the most perfectly wonderful person I could imagine. The bad news was that, once I realized my Jesus was merely a projection of my own ideals, he lost all authority in my life.

Of course, while today's Christians often disagree about what Jesus would do here and now, they are remarkably unified about the supreme importance of what he did, once and for all, two thousand years ago at Calvary. Indeed, virtually every Christian believes that the Cross is the foundation of his or her salvation, and that the redemptive grace it expresses is the most wonderful part of the Gospel. Certainly my father believes these things. As he often says, without the perfect sacrifice of Jesus's crucifixion and the decisive victory over sin and death of Jesus's resurrection, the rest of his theology falls apart. As the apostle Paul once put it, if Christ is not risen, then he and his fellow believers are of all people most to be pitied, for their faith is in vain (1 Corinthians 15:14, 18).

Unfortunately, like the students in my father's seminar, I can't buy his Jesus story, and even when I did, I secretly despised big chunks of it. To me, the essence of the Apostles' Creed—that Jesus was conceived by the Holy Spirit; born of the virgin Mary; suffered under Pontius Pilate; was crucified, dead, and buried; descended to hell; rose again from the dead; and ascended to heaven to sit at his Father's right hand—seems like quite the opposite of good news. In fact, as far as I am concerned, the notion that God requires a blood sacrifice to forgive the sins of humanity is easily the saddest, most hurtful, and most discouraging doctrine ever invented.

Original sin is where the Gospel starts, isn't it? Whether Adam and Eve were literal or metaphorical, the consequence of their transgression is that all the rest of us are conceived and born into sin, unworthy of fellowship with the holiness of God. We are all sinful by nature, and therefore utterly incapable of redeeming ourselves and entirely deserving of eternal damnation. Once you get used to the idea, you can pick your own biblical moniker for us: filthy rags, objects of wrath, infidels, children of disobedience, God's enemies.

It doesn't make sense to me that we should think about ourselves this way, let alone that the loving God who made us should do so. I get it that we aren't perfect, or sometimes even much good, but I've still never met anyone who was utterly depraved, without even a drop of humanity left. More importantly, I know lots of people who quite obviously do not deserve eternal damnation. I'm not just talking about big-ticket heroes like Mother Teresa or Nelson Mandela, either, but also everyday folks who love their friends and family and who most often try to do the right thing. We all know people like that. We all know some little children too, and no matter how badly they misbehave, we wouldn't condemn a single one to burn in hell. So then, why would God?

This may well be my biggest problem with evangelical Christianity: It is grounded in a bizarre, counterintuitive self-hatred that claims we have no intrinsic goodness or value of our own, but rather deserve to be eternally punished simply for being born human. Indeed, according to the "good news," our only hope is the unmerited favor of God, which comes to us in the form of Jesus, the sacrificial lamb who suffers and dies in our place.

I mean really, even if we do need to be forgiven by God for being born human and falling short of moral perfection, why must anyone be murdered in the process? Why can't our gracious God simply forgive us, the same way Jesus taught his disciples to forgive one another? Again, the whole setup makes no sense. I mean, we human beings forgive one another all the time, most often without even demanding an eye for an eye, let alone torturing and killing those who trespass against us. Moreover, we certainly wouldn't torture and kill a blameless bystander in order to justify letting the real culprit off the hook. What good would that do, anyway? How could slaughtering an innocent make the guilty party any more fit for divine fellowship? Parental discipline I can easily accept, but not the retributive violence of the Cross. To me, that is what's really immoral.

NOT SO FAST: WHY SECULARISTS SHOULD TAKE ANOTHER LOOK AT THE CROSS

by Tony Campolo

TOWARD THE END OF my academic career, a new theological movement called the emerging church began shaking the very bedrock of evangelical theology. Influential writers such as Brian McLaren and Tony Jones publicly asked hard questions about the doctrine of penal substitutionary atonement. This doctrine has been a hallmark of Protestantism going back to the time of the Reformation, especially in the works of Martin Luther and John Calvin, and there is much biblical support for it. Simply stated, it goes like this:

- All human beings are sinners.
- A just and holy God must and will punish us sinners with death.
- Jesus, the sinless Son of God, willingly offers Himself as a substitute to die in our place on Calvary's cross.
- The shed blood of Christ forever cleanses us from all unrighteousness, rendering us fit for heaven.

Many leaders of the emerging church are repelled by the idea that God is a bloodthirsty deity who, like the ancient pagan gods, requires blood sacrifices to be appeased. Beyond that, like Bart, they argue that a just God would never punish an innocent person in place of the guilty. In England, prominent evangelist Steve Chalke has gone even further, shocking the British evangelical community by declaring that requiring His own son to suffer a tortuous crucifixion would make God no less than a cosmic child abuser.

My response to such leaders has been to point out that the penal substitutionary doctrine of the atonement is only one explanation of how our salvation was accomplished by Jesus on the cross, and to remind them that none of them alone can contain the whole story. What happened at Calvary is far too profound to be reduced to a simple formula. I do not reject penal substitutionary atonement out of hand, but I don't put all my theological eggs in that basket, either. The glory of our salvation is bigger than that. As an old hymn puts it:

> Could we with ink the ocean fill,
> And were the sky of parchment made;
> Were every stalk on earth a quill,
> And every man a scribe by trade;
> To write the love of God above
> Would drain the ocean dry;
> Nor could the scroll contain the whole,
> Though stretched from sky to sky.

—"The Love of God," Frederick M. Lehman (1917)

As Bart well knows, I have my own special way of reflecting on Calvary, which enables me to experience a spiritual cleansing that alleviates the burden of sin and guilt that would otherwise overwhelm me. Almost every night, I lie in bed and intently focus on Jesus as He hangs from the cross, in order to emotionally, psychologically, and spiritually connect with Him. In that moment I surrender to the suffering Christ and wait for Him to reach out to me in empathy. A kind of transference takes place, as I let go of all my failures and the ugliness in my heart, and wait for Him to draw those things from me and absorb them into Himself. Jesus, hanging on the cross, is like a magnet, and my sins are like iron filings being pulled out of me, across time and space, into Him.

In this way of thinking, I am much like Søren Kierkegaard, the Danish existentialist, who once described Christ on the cross as the "eternally crucified." Like most Christians, Kierkegaard understood that Jesus was and is both fully human and fully divine. *In His humanity,* He died at a particular place and at a particular time. *In His divinity,* however, Jesus transcends history. As Salvador Dalí's great crucifixion painting suggests, the crucified Christ hangs above the linear progression of time and thus is able to reach out and connect with each and every one of us, at every moment in our lives, offering His light in exchange for our darkness. As it says in the King James Bible, *"For he hath made him to be sin for us, who knew no sin; that we might be made the righteousness of God in him"* (2 Corinthians 5:21). Or as a Russian Orthodox friend of mine once put it, "On the cross He became everything that we are, so that we might become everything that He is."

Ironically, it is none other than Albert Einstein who lends

some legitimacy to this explanation of our salvation, in his famous theory of relativity.

Up until the development of Einsteinian physics, it was assumed that in all places and in all situations and circumstances, time would be experienced in exactly the same manner. If there were creatures with consciousness throughout the universe, it was believed that they all would be experiencing the same inexorable flow of time. We thought that whether a conscious creature was on Earth or on some planet in a solar system located in a galaxy billions of light-years away, the passage of a day would be experienced in the same way. However, such commonsense thinking was challenged and refuted when Einstein proposed and gave evidence for his new theory.

The new physics of Einstein challenges us to understand that time is relative to motion. The faster I travel relative to you, the more slowly time will pass relative to you. Let's put it this way: If I were to get into a rocket ship and travel into space at the speed of 130,000 miles per second relative to the people on this planet, with instructions to travel for ten years before returning, I would, upon coming back to Earth, find that I had aged ten years while everyone and everything on Earth had aged twenty years. With me traveling at that speed, twenty years of your time would transpire in ten years of mine. If I could travel 150,000 miles per second relative to you, a thousand years of your time would be compressed into what I would experience in a day. And if I could travel at the speed of light (186,000 miles per second), then all of human history and the history of the planet itself would be compressed into a moment that has no extension of time and could properly be called "an eternal now."

An experiment conducted at the physics research laboratory

of Princeton University involved studying the effects of rapid speed on a hydrogen atom set in motion in a cyclotron. The hydrogen atom traveled at speeds that approximated 32,000 miles per second. That was the highest speed at which the atom could travel while still providing scientists the possibility of observing its pulsation rate (that is, the rate at which the electron circles the nucleus of the atom). As the relative speed of the atom increased, this rate of pulsation slowed down. The speed at which the electron circled the nucleus of the atom decreased. At least, that's the way it appeared to the scientists observing this phenomenon. If the atom itself had consciousness, it would not perceive that it had slowed down, but instead would perceive that the world of the scientist had sped up.

Time is relative to motion, and at the speed of light, time as an inexorable flow of successive events ceases to exist at all. At the speed of light, everything is caught up in an eternal now. The temporal is caught up in the eternal. It is difficult to pull all of this together, especially for those of us whose categories of thinking are not adapted to an Einsteinian perspective on reality. However, the more I read in the field of contemporary astrophysics, the more I am convinced that "now" is part of eternity and that eternity can be experienced now. I am led to believe that what I encounter now does not simply become part of dead history, but is part of an eternal now that belongs to another level of existence.

I believe God comprehends the entire universe that way. For God, everything happens *now*. Indeed, God's self-description— "I am that I am"—implies that very timelessness. God never was and never will be, because both past and present are gathered together into God's eternal now. That is why the Bible tells us that with God, a thousand years are as a day, and a day is as a thousand years (2 Peter 3:8). And that is why Jesus could say, *"Before Abraham was, I am."*

In His humanity, Jesus apprehended time as a linear progression of events, but in His divinity, Christ was and is able to squeeze all of linear time into His eternal now. Therefore, although Jesus Christ hung on the cross two thousand years ago, He is forever simultaneous with every single person in time and history. That's why He can connect with me each night as I yield to Him. Lying in bed, I feel Him reaching out across time and space, not only to absorb my sin and doubt but also to pour His righteousness into me. The Bible makes plain that through Jesus, God imputes this same righteousness to every human being who has spiritually surrendered to Him. That means salvation not only reaches those of us who came after His resurrection but also extends back in time to include those who trusted God before Jesus was born.

Obviously, these thoughts carry me beyond the problems of those who question the character of God implied by the penal substitutionary doctrine of the atonement.

This doctrine, first articulated by St. Augustine and later laid out with greater clarity by St. Anselm, provides us believers with some valuable insights about the glorious happenings on that first Good Friday, but it only scratches the surface. I have offered my combination of Kierkegaard's Christology and Einstein's theory of relativity not to propose a formal addition to evangelical theology, but only to explain how I respond to the harsh critiques of those who, like my son, Bart, have found the traditional teachings of Calvin and Luther to be a hindrance to faith.

Of course, Bart's problems are not only with Reformed theological interpretations of the Bible, but also with what he considers its many scientific errors and internal contradictions. Like many skeptics, he has compiled a long list of Old Testament verses suggesting a flat earth, a Ptolemaic cosmology, and a six-day Creation, to which he has added a variety of New Testament accounts that don't even agree with one another, let alone the historical record.

My response to such "problems" is simple: They don't really matter. Sure, if you try to read it literally, the Bible contains some mistakes and inaccuracies, but that is not how its ancient authors expected it to be read, and that is not how it has been read by Christians for hundreds and hundreds of years. In fact, the idea that the Bible is literally and inerrantly true is a relatively new one, introduced at the beginning of the twentieth century by a small group of American Protestants in a series of tracts called "The Fundamentals." Unfortunately, those fundamentalists and their followers have led lots of people—including lots of skeptics—into reading the Bible the wrong way.

As I see it, the Gospel writers were not as interested in the details of Jesus's life as they were in the truth of it. Like their Old Testament counterparts, they carefully constructed their stories to give their readers insights about the meaning and purpose of life. To ask if this or that really happened the way it's described is to miss the point. What matters isn't whether each of those accounts is scrupulously accurate and consistent with all the others. What matters is what they collectively reveal about the nature of God.

For example, the Gospel of Matthew says that Jesus was born in 4 BC, while the Gospel of Luke says it happened in AD 6. A skeptic might say that that ten-year discrepancy invalidates the Christmas story, but to me such nitpicking seems silly. Think about it. Surely the church fathers who canonized both Matthew and Luke must have read them first. Surely they must have noticed those two different dates for Jesus's birth, along with Matthew's and Luke's completely different genealogies for Jesus. They left them that way because they knew better than to think or care about whether what they were reading was factually accurate. All that mattered was that it rang true.

When I seek the truths that scripture reveals to me, I do so in the way that St. Ignatius called *lectio divina*. In my daily devotional life, I do not approach the Bible like some kind of textbook, but rather carefully meditate on what I have read. I go over a passage of scripture several times, praying for God to show me what I need to glean from it. Before His ascension, Jesus told his disciples He would send the Holy Spirit to teach us all things and remind us of what He said (John 14:26), and I daily rely on that promise. As I surrender to the Spirit's leading, truths emerge from the words I am reading that are much more profound than a merely literal reading would yield.

Frankly, if Bart read the Bible the way I do, openly searching for spiritual realities instead of comparing and contrasting the empirical data, I think he might find that it still rings true, especially when it comes to the rest of Jesus's story. After all, it really is the greatest story ever told.

Godless Goodness:
The Foundations of a
Secular Morality

by Bart Campolo

I APPRECIATE MY FATHER'S WAY around my problems with the Cross, which enables him to hang on to God the Father as the ultimate source of human morality, and Jesus as both its perfect example and its enabling force. As far as I'm concerned, however, morality is just another place where we human beings are better off on our own. It isn't just that the Ten Commandments are problematic, or that we can't really know Jesus in the first place, or even that the negative implications of the Cross are so awful, but when it comes to figuring out what's right and wrong, we've had a way better source code since long before he was born.

Unfortunately, no matter how articulate a secularist may be on other issues, he or she is apt to become suddenly tongue-tied when asked where his or her sense of right and wrong comes from. I feel that way myself sometimes, even though I've had plenty of practice explaining my morals to religious people who can't fathom the idea of being good without God. When I'm on my game, however, here's my basic explanation:

On a personal level, like nearly everyone who is fair, kind, and considerate of others, I was raised by fair, kind, and considerate adults who taught me the basics of human empathy by both word and deed. As in many households, in many places, for many thousands of years, those basics were simply summarized for me in the Golden Rule: Do unto others as you would have them do unto you. As a little boy, long before I heard any Christian teachings about sex, drugs, alcohol, money, or idolatry, I was made to understand that the essence of being a good person had to do with not harming other people on the one hand and doing your best to help them on the other.

While some might argue that the Golden Rule itself is a Christian teaching, the ancient Egyptians wrote it down more than five hundred years before Jesus was born, as did Confucius in China and Thales in Greece and Siddhartha in India. Later, but still before Jesus, Rabbi Hillel taught the same precept to his followers in the Holy Land, and versions of it appear in virtually all of the rest of the world's great religions. Ironically, none of these faith traditions supposes that any kind of supernatural revelation is required for human beings to know how to treat one another. When it comes to morality, it seems, virtually everyone knows all we really need is everyday human empathy.

I don't mean to be trite, but everyday human empathy is exactly what my parents and the other important adults in my life taught, both implicitly and explicitly, every day of my childhood. First of all—and I can't emphasize this enough—nobody ever verbally, emotionally, sexually, or physically abused me, even when I acted out. While I am not suggesting that survivors of such childhood traumas cannot and do not become warm, caring, morally upright adults, there is no question that abuse, neglect, and abandonment complicate the development of empathy. So too does any form of authoritarianism that doesn't allow for weakness and forgive mistakes.

In my case, even when I misbehaved, I was very seldom disciplined according to a hard and fast set of rules. Instead, my wrongdoing was always explained to me in terms of the harm it did to other people, and I was most often punished or rewarded on the basis of how I made someone else feel. I was constantly encouraged to notice other people, to imagine what it might feel like to be in their situations. "How would you enjoy it if someone treated you that way?," I was asked over and over again. What was praiseworthy in my family had little to do with blind obedience; it was all about thoughtfully showing kindness and respect toward those around us, and especially to those in need. Not surprisingly, that's how I tried to raise my kids as well, and how I hope they'll raise theirs.

Of course, all the best moral teaching in the world can't make a person fundamentally fair, kind, and considerate if that person's genes and hormones don't cooperate. While I certainly had loads of positive early childhood experiences, clearly I also had a brain capable of learning, remembering, and imagining, without which I never would have developed empathy, the critical ingredient of moral goodness. We have all encountered or at least heard of children whose brains are dysfunctional or damaged in ways that keep them from forming significant attachments or genuinely caring about the feelings of other people, and we intuitively understand the tragic consequences of such conditions. As grateful as I am for the moral influence of my family, I am just as grateful that I had enough mental health to take advantage of it.

I also had the luxury of spending my childhood in stable conditions where, on a practical level, the Golden Rule worked perfectly well for me and everyone I knew. Indeed, as far as I could tell, the people I depended on never had to lie, cheat, steal, or use any kind of violence to protect and provide for me. I was kept safe, warm, and well fed from the very beginning, and the other families in my church and neighborhood generally took for granted the same moral values and privileges as my own. Obviously, not everyone is born so lucky.

All over the world, little boys and girls grow up in the midst of extreme poverty, violence, and injustice and must learn a very different moral code in order to survive. I don't like calling the Golden Rule a luxury item, but I have certainly known parents who quite literally could not afford to follow or even think much about it, let alone teach it to their children. Sadly, in places where chaos reigns, the rule of the jungle works better for taking care of your family. That's why a street kid in a slum in Port-au-Prince, Haiti, is almost certain to develop a very different sense of what is right and wrong about stealing and sharing than the one I learned in my leafy Main Line suburb.

Our morality doesn't come just from our families, either, but also from what we as children experience in the wider world around us. I saw this most clearly when I worked with human rights activists in the occupied West Bank, where Israeli settlers and Palestinian villagers live a stone's throw apart in utterly different realities. Why respect authority when the powers that be routinely arrest and terrorize your friends in the name of keeping the peace? Why refrain from violence when neighbors openly threaten to unleash violence on your children? I quickly learned that your answers to such questions—not to mention your image of God—largely depended on which side of the conflict you lived when growing up.

I reference the Israeli-Palestinian conflict here on purpose, as a reminder that moral development is just one part of that much larger process sociologists like my father call socialization, whereby we human beings learn to understand and interpret ourselves and our lives not only from our families and neighbors but also from the cultural norms and values that surround and define us. Religion is an important part of any given culture, of course, but so is every other human construction, like language, trade, agriculture, marriage, medicine, technology, colonialism, and warfare. Each culture has a somewhat different moral code, and all of them—including American evangelical Christianity—are relentlessly changing over time. So then, for better or worse, my understanding of right and wrong was as much a function of where and when I was born as it is of how I was raised.

What it wasn't a function of, however, was anything objectively justifiable. Honestly, I am always mystified when Christians ask me how I can trust any moral code not grounded on the fixed and absolute moral authority of God. That's exactly the point I've been trying to make: Nobody decides to trust a moral code because it is objectively justifiable or divinely inspired. In fact, nobody decides to trust a moral code at all. We don't choose our understandings of right and wrong and where they come from. We absorb those things as children, and only rationalize them for ourselves and one another long after the fact.

I understand the gut-level attraction of the idea that almighty God defines good and evil, but it's awfully hard for me to swallow. I mean, are things like rape and murder evil simply because God forbids them, or are they objectively wrong? Regardless, isn't morality really about thinking through the potential impact of my actions, weighing the various options against a complex matrix of competing values, and humbly making the best decision possible? For me to blindly follow a divine commandment seems like a way to shirk the hard work of deliberation and evade responsibility for the intentions and consequences of my actions. Simple obedience might keep people of faith from doing bad things, but I'm not sure how it helps them become morally good themselves. Unless, of course, your definition of goodness is to blindly trust and obey, rather than to thoughtfully figure out what fairness, kindness, and consideration look like in any given situation.

Bringing God into the equation also confuses things when it comes to the underlying motivations for our moral decisions. After all, is an act of will really moral if you only undertake it to win God's favor or avoid God's wrath? Whose moral character do you admire most—the person who does the right thing in order to gain rewards or avoid punishments, or the person who does it based on their understanding of what's at stake for everyone, because they find doing right intrinsically fulfilling? It seems to me that goodness not done for goodness' sake alone might not be truly good at all. Again, when it comes to personal morality, I vastly prefer the no-God simplicity of the Golden Rule.

Another thing I like about the Golden Rule is that, thanks to Charles Darwin and his colleagues, we have a pretty good idea of where it comes from and why it is so consistent across cultures throughout human history. Indeed, there isn't much question that our moral instincts—beginning with empathy—are a product of evolution by natural selection.

Here's how it works: Every living organism has self-replicating material called DNA that determines its physical characteristics. Occasionally the DNA in an organism sponta-neously mutates in a way that causes changes in its offspring, which are harmful, neutral, or helpful. If the change is harmful, the offspring is less likely to survive to reproduce, so the muta-tion eventually dies out. If the change is helpful, however, the offspring thrive and reproduce more offspring, and the mutation spreads. Eventually, over long periods of time, the mutant and nonmutant forms of the original organism separate into differ-ent species, which is why after many millions of years there are so many varieties of life on this planet, from single-celled bac-teria all the way up to us incredibly complicated human beings.

I'm no evolutionary anthropologist, but when it comes to morality, I think the most important DNA mutation of all time must be the one that separated the first of us mammals from our reptilian ancestors. After all, while reptilian brains work just fine when it comes to managing hunger, temperature control, fight-or-flight fear responses, reproduction, and the other basics of survival, they have no capacity for memory or emotion. We mammals, on the other hand, have added to those reptilian in-stincts what biologists call the limbic system, which enables us to feel emotions, remember experiences, and cooperate with one another as a survival strategy. Because more complicated brains take longer to fully develop, however, mammals can't take care of themselves at birth, and therefore must be nurtured by their mothers. That is where empathy begins, evolutionarily speaking, with the natural selection of those first females who noticed when their offspring were cold, hungry, or endangered, and responded to their needs in ways that kept them alive.

Evidence for the evolution of maternal empathy—which quickly spreads to other relationships—appears in our heads, where our brains produce and process the oxytocin, endorphins, and other hormones associated with cooperative relationships. It also appears in the interactions of the chimpanzees and bonobos studied by primatologist Frans de Waal, who points out that human beings are not the only animals that love, fear, share with, steal from, hold grudges against, forgive, miss, and ultimately grieve one another. On the contrary, many social animals live in highly structured groups where rules and inhibitions, competition and cooperation, and petty selfishness and acts of genuine kindness are everyday realities. What emerges in such groups is the most basic rule of every moral code: Behaviors that cause the group to thrive are rewarded with food, sex, status, or some other benefit, while behaviors that harm the group are punished with violence or shunning, or some other immediate penalty.

What sets us human beings apart, de Waal suggests, is the later development of an additional part of our brain, the prefrontal cortex, where we reason, think logically, recognize the passage of time, generalize our experiences, and make complex decisions. Our prefrontal cortexes are what enable us to extend primitive moral intuitions into universal standards of behavior—like the Golden Rule—and combine them with increasingly elaborate systems of justification, monitoring, and punishment. That's where religion comes in, of course, when a group gets too big to reinforce its values the old-fashioned way, and must invent powerful supernatural enforcers with eyes in the sky to keep us in line. As de Waal puts it in his *The Bonobo and the Atheist: In Search of Humanism Among the Primates* (2013), "It wasn't God who introduced us to morality; rather, it was the other way around. God was put into place to help us live the way we felt we ought to."

Forgive me for getting so technical here, especially when all I'm really trying to say is that I'm pretty sure there is no objective justification for human morality. Rather than being handed down in the Ten Commandments, the Five Pillars of Islam, the Eightfold Path of Buddhism, or any other divine revelation, I think our deep sense of right and wrong has naturally grown up betwixt and between us as we've interacted over time in order to survive. Moreover, because that process is ongoing, I believe that besides being essentially subjective, human morality is also a moving target. The only constant, as far as I can tell, is that in the end we all define moral goodness according to whatever makes our own group flourish.

If I'm right, then it makes sense that so many norms, mores, and values are similar across cultures, because there are some laws of nature that apply equally around the world. Antisocial behaviors like lying, murder, and incest don't work for anyone under any circumstances over the long run, so they are universally proscribed.

Of course, if group flourishing is truly the ultimate standard of goodness, then it also makes sense that rules about food, water, sexuality, child-rearing, and other aspects of community life would vary widely from group to group, depending on the conditions under which they develop. Even so, all such rules are ultimately rooted in mutual care and responsibility in the context of cooperative groups. Simply stated, human morality is and always has been fundamentally about human relationships.

That's why we naturally feel different levels of moral obligation to other people depending on how closely related we are. Your immediate family members—and especially your children—are your primary concern; you'll look out for them over and against anyone else in your tribe, just as you'll look out for the other members of your tribe over and against anyone in the rest of your country, and your country over and against the rest of the world.

Biologically speaking, we're loyal that way because each of us instinctively grasps that our own well-being is wrapped up in the well-being of those closest to us. Indeed, the process of evolution has wonderfully equipped us to frequently blur the lines between our own health and happiness and the health and happiness of those we care about. That's why we don't need any fixed and absolute divine authority upon which to base our moral judgments; good old everyday human empathy does just fine. To set in stone any commandment more specific than the Golden Rule would be to ignore the fact that circumstances on this planet are constantly changing and, more importantly, to abdicate our natural responsibility to thoughtfully protect our species, our country, our community, and, above all, our own children.

AND THEN WHAT? WHY SECULARISTS CAN'T FACE DEATH

by Tony Campolo

FOR THE SECULARIST, EVERYTHING is temporal. All things pass away. Every creature dies. There is no everlasting life, and nothing is eternal. Life is a purely natural phenomenon, and when the biological process has run its course, death is the natural conclusion. There is no heaven; there is no hell; there is no afterlife. In the end, there is nothing at all. It is difficult to face up to this reality, of course, and down through the ages men have sought ways to evade it. Religion, according to the secular thinker, is sometimes deliberately invented in order to offer the hope of an afterlife to those who lack the courage to face up to their own finitude. To the humanist, belief in an afterlife is nothing more than wishful thinking. He or she may try to be brave in making these assertions, but beneath the surface, I believe we all suffer from profound fears and anxieties.

Young people often refuse to face the fact that they too will die one day. This makes it easier for them to talk about death.

I was often amused at the apparent ease with which my secular students could proclaim that this life is all there is, but it is hard for young collegians to comprehend their own mortality and grasp the significance of their own finitude. To them, dying is something that happens to old people. It doesn't happen to them and their friends. Logically, they know that one day they will die, but they live so detached from this fact that it barely affects them. They live as though their time will last forever and there will always be another tomorrow. Looking at the clock that never stops, it is easy for them to delude themselves into thinking that for them there is no end of time. Perhaps it was better when we measured time with hourglasses, for then even our young were always reminded that time runs out.

Many years ago, I led a course on existentialism. One by one, I asked each student to share the effects that the knowledge of their impending death had upon the way in which they lived. In this class, largely made up of young students, there was only one middle-aged woman. She waited until last to speak and began by gently but firmly telling the others that they didn't know what they were talking about.

She continued, "One time I went to an organ concert where one of the keys got stuck. At first, I hardly noticed it. It was only during the pauses in the music that one could faintly hear its sound. But as the concert progressed, the sound of the stuck note got louder and louder until it was no longer possible to enjoy the music. That one note ruined everything.

"That's the way the reality of death has affected me. When I was younger, I only thought about it at those times when I had nothing else to think about. In the melancholy pauses of my existence, I would reflect on the fact that someday I might die. But as the years passed, the awareness of my death became more and more pronounced. I came to be aware of it not only during the pauses but also in the midst of my routine activities. Eventually that awareness became so powerful that it has permeated everything I do and think, and rendered me incapable of enjoying anything."

The class fell silent. They knew that this woman was right— they did not understand the power of death.

Like those students, secularists claim that at the other end of life there is nothing, but they sometimes fail to see that one cannot face this prospect with neutrality. The nothingness rushes toward them and passes judgment on everything that they have done or tried. They know that their lofty dreams, their greatest achievements, and their meaningful experiences will all be erased. As death approaches, they sense a futility to everything. As a mentor of mine once put it, "We make so much noise on New Year's Eve because we are trying to drown out the macabre sound of grass growing over our own graves."

Likewise, Søren Kierkegaard compared life to a smooth, flat stone thrown over the surface of a pond. The stone dances and skims over the surface of the water until that moment comes when like life itself, it runs out of momentum and sinks into nothingness.

One existentialist, Martin Heidegger, endeavors to see some positive consequences arising from the nihilistic view of temporal existence that typifies the secular mind-set. Heidegger argues that Christianity cheapens life in this world by suggesting that it is only a prelude to a richer and better eternal life after death. If this is true, then earthly existence need not really be taken seriously. Heidegger condemns this belief because it keeps people from realizing the ultimate significance of every moment of every day. The Christian doctrine of eternal life diminishes the need for people to passionately live this life to the fullest. According to Heidegger, it leaves people unappreciative of life.

Such unappreciative people populate Thornton Wilder's familiar classic *Our Town,* in which Emily Webb, the play's main character, discovers too late the singular joy of just being alive. In act 3, after Emily's death, the Stage Manager allows her to watch herself relive one day of her life. She is warned that she will not enjoy what she experiences. Nevertheless, she embraces the opportunity and chooses her twelfth birthday. Seeing the way her family members take one another for granted and live with so little passion is so painful for her that she finally pleads to be delivered from it all. Looking back one last time, Emily cries out, "Oh, earth, you're too wonderful for anybody to realize you." She stops, hesitates, and then, with tears in her eyes, asks the audience, "Do any human beings realize life while they live it?—every, every minute?"

Heidegger believes that until a person comes to grips with their own death and realizes its consequences, they are not capable of realizing life in a way that does it justice. It is only in the face of death that they become fully alive, because it is only in the face of death that they address themselves to life with the glorious intensity that makes them fully human.

I must admit that Heidegger's warnings make a great deal of sense to me. In fact, I have revised my theology about what happens when I die so that my view of the afterlife can contribute to the meaning of my life here and now. Perhaps I can best explain my view of the Christian doctrine of eternal life by another illustration from my teaching experience.

One day in class, I asked my students a simple question: "How long have you lived?" The students had no idea what I was driving at and seemed irritated that I would waste their time with such a trivial question. Nevertheless, they answered me. One of them said he had lived twenty-two years; another, twenty-one; and so on.

"No, no!" I responded. "I didn't ask you how long you have existed. I asked you how long you have lived. There is a big difference between living and existing. You may have existed for twenty-two years, but you have lived very few moments. Most of your life has been a meaningless passage of time between isolated instances when you were fully alive.

"When I was twelve years old, my school class was taken to New York City. Among the things we did there was to take a ride to the top of the Empire State Building. Thirty-five of us raced around the walkway at the top of the huge edifice. We played tag. We shouted and screamed at each other; we all were having a great deal of fun. Then, for some reason that I don't understand, I suddenly stopped. I walked over to the rail of the walkway, grasped it tightly, and stared at the awesome expanse of Manhattan below me. I concentrated on the scene with great intensity. I focused all my energies on creating a memory of what I was experiencing. I wanted to fix it in my mind forever. I experienced the scene that lay before me with a heightened awareness. I could live for a million years and that experience would still be a part of me. That moment was lifted out of time and eternalized.

"I'm sure you know what it's like to capture a moment like that. Perhaps you were with your lover. The ecstasy of lovemaking made the moment so precious that you wanted to hold on to it forever. The separation between you and your lover was overcome, and you sensed a oneness as fulfilling as any experience described by religious gurus. You know what I mean when I talk about eternalized moments. You've lived some of them and long to live many more. Now let me ask again. How long have you lived?"

There was silence in the class, and then one student said, "If you put together all the moments in which I was fully alive, I lived maybe a minute, maybe less. I guess I haven't lived very much at all."

My belief about the afterlife is that when I die, I will carry to the other side of the grave all of the moments that I have eternalized during my natural existence. This means that every moment of every day has ultimate significance, for each moment has the potentiality of being eternalized. Every human experience has the possibility of being lifted out of time and made part of everlasting life. I find it a moral imperative to take life seriously, to live it intensely, to taste it passionately, and to enjoy it fully. To do otherwise would be to allow my life to be nothing more than "hay, wood, and stubble," which will be consumed and reduced to nothing when my time on earth is over. However, if I live with the kind of passion that Heidegger suggests, if I live with total awareness and "redeem the time," then at death all of that will remain with me. I believe that in the afterlife we will freely share our eternalized experiences with one another. Heaven will be an intense give-and-take of ecstatic moments that last forever.

I have found that there are two conditions that prevent me from experiencing this life as my theology dictates. The first is guilt, and the second is anxiety. Guilt keeps me oriented to the past. It focuses my attention on the things I should have done, and the things I should not have done. Guilt is a burden that saps my energy, dissipates my enthusiasm for life, and destroys my appetite for savoring the fullness of each moment. Anxiety, on the other hand, orients me to the future and keeps me from enjoying life in the present, because of the dread that I have about the future. Caught between guilt over the past and anxiety over the future, I have nothing left with which to address the present moment in which I find myself.

When I meet people, they are sometimes left with the feeling that I am absent, that I am "not really there." Despite my physical presence, I am really somewhere else in time and space. That's why I need Jesus.

The Gospel is the good news that Jesus delivers me from my guilt, and the past no longer need torture me. I am not simply referring to the biblical fact that Jesus died on the cross for my sins, and so I need not fear that my sinful past will catch up with me. More important, the Jesus declared in scripture is one whom I mystically encounter, who invades my personhood, and who provides an inner deliverance. My sin is forgiven and forgotten, buried in the deepest sea and remembered no more. Any who read the testimonies of Christian converts will discover, over and over again, references to the wonderful freedom from guilt that accompanies their new life in Christ.

But there is further good news declared in the proclamation of the Gospel. Jesus not only delivers me from the effects of yesterday's sin but also delivers me from the anxiety that makes me reluctant to face the future. The old cliché suddenly becomes meaningful as I recognize that "I do not know what the future holds, but I know who holds the future."

To be saved is to have a relationship with Jesus that frees me from guilt and anxiety so that I can live each moment with the eternalized quality that scripture promises to the sons and daughters of God. This is what it means to be "born again" into everlasting life.

Don't get me wrong—however many eternalized moments each of us brings from this life, I believe an even more wonderful eternity awaits everybody who trusts Jesus as their personal Lord and Savior. Yes, I know that the doctrines of bodily resurrection and eternal life defy science, reason, and empirical verification, and yes, I remain convinced that they are true nevertheless. The fact that I cannot prove it doesn't keep me and my Christian brothers and sisters from gathering on Easter to declare, "Christ is risen! He is risen, indeed!"

It is not surprising that secular humanists like Bart doubt our convictions, but here is something to bear in mind: On a pragmatic level, they don't have a very good track record when it comes to dealing with death. For obvious reasons, they have few good answers to the emotional and psychological pain that so often accompanies the existential threat of nonbeing.

Bart probably remembers that his grandfather Robert Davidson brilliantly conquered that pain in his dying moments. Suffering from dementia, this old preacher had long ago lost the ability to carry on a conversation, but nevertheless he kept his faith. As Bart's grandmother told it, she woke up at five o'clock one morning to find her husband sitting up in bed, firmly rebuking an unseen presence. "O death, where is thy sting?" he said. "O grave, where is thy victory?" Three times he cried out this way, each time stronger and louder. Finally, with a triumphant flourish, he declared, "Thanks be to God, who giveth us the victory through our Lord Jesus Christ!," fell back into the bed, and died. What a good way to go.

My mother died more quietly, but only after writing a letter to her family and friends, affirming her assurance of eternal life, along with instructions for the invitation and altar call for her funeral. This good woman, who had to drop out of school in the eighth grade to support her immigrant family, closed her final message with joyful confidence. "I'm finally graduating!" she wrote. "Be happy for me."

I probably won't be around when Bart's time comes, but when it does, I worry that his secular clarity will not serve him as well as his grandparents' faith.

Let me be clear—when I say "Bart's time," I am not referring to Judgment Day, but rather to that moment when the awareness of his own mortality threatens to overwhelm him in the way my middle-aged student described to her younger classmates. Old as I am, I've had my share of such moments, but it is the first one I remember best. I was just thirty-one, a happily married father of two small children with a clean bill of health, but none of that mattered. One night, as I laid my head on my pillow, I suddenly had the most terrifying realization. "Tony," I said to myself, "you're one day closer." A tremor ran up my spine, but I couldn't move. I hated that thought and did my best to suppress it, but it didn't go away until—you guessed it—I started to pray.

Part of the Bargain: Facing Death the Secular Humanist Way

by Bart Campolo

When I was a kid, my older cousin Ray was more full of life than anyone else I knew. Once he became a student at Eastern University, I saw him all the time, and he quickly became my hero. I often tagged along with the local youth group he led because, as another kid put it, "Anyplace Ray goes is an instant party." Ray stayed like that—smart, funny, kind, and charismatic—all the way through college and seminary and into the pastorate, until one day, when he was just forty-two, he suffered a massive stroke that left him brain-dead.

I remember sitting with my Aunt Ann after she agreed to let the doctors turn off Ray's ventilator and harvest his organs, watching him die and desperately wanting to believe that somehow, somewhere, we'd see him again. Until that moment, heaven was just a fairy tale to me, but suddenly I needed to believe it was real. That's only natural, I think, whether or not you are a Christian. Robert Ingersoll, who in the late nineteenth century was widely regarded as America's greatest orator, put it this way:

> *The idea of immortality, that like a sea has ebbed and flowed in the*
> *human heart, with its countless waves of hope and fear, beating against*
> *the shores and rocks of time and fate, was not born of any book, nor*
> *of any creed, nor of any religion. It was born of human affection, and*
> *it will continue to ebb and flow beneath the mists and clouds of doubt*
> *and darkness as long as love kisses the lips of death. It is the rain-*
> *bow—Hope, shining upon the tears of grief.*

> —*The Works of Robert G. Ingersoll*, 2012

That observation—that religions didn't invent the human hope of eternal life, but rather vice versa—resonates with my own experience. Over and over again, I hear grieving people console themselves and one another with the promise that their loved one isn't really dead at all, but only in another, better place where they will all be happily and permanently reunited in due time.

At such moments, of course, it is not my place to point out that wishing for something doesn't make it true, or that there is no convincing evidence of life after death. On the contrary, the older I get, the less prone I am to dispute heaven with believers even when all is calm. After all, wanting eternal life is only natural. Still, Ingersoll questions it:

> *There is one thing of which I am certain, and that is, that if we could*
> *live forever here, we would care nothing for each other. The fact that*
> *we must die, the fact that the feast must end, brings our souls together,*
> *and treads the weeds from out the paths between our hearts.*

Anyone who has spent much time in a hospital or hospice recognizes this truth. When people know that their time is short, they long to be surrounded by those who matter most to them. Often they say important things—thank you, I'm sorry, I'm proud of you, please forgive me, promise me this, I love you—that should have been said long ago. Relationships are reconciled. Grudges are finally forgotten. Healing happens. Thanks and affirmations flow freely. And all of us wonder: *Why did it take so long?*

In fact, such goodness is not a function of time but rather of its sure and certain end. Without the impending separation of death, there would be no urgency for us to connect or reconnect. *I'll do it tomorrow,* we would say to ourselves. *I'll do it next week. Or next month. I'll do it a hundred, or a thousand, or a million years from now.* Eternity is the enemy. Like it or not, love needs a deadline.

That's my big problem with the fantasy of heaven: It distracts people from the most important reality of life on earth.

Like every commodity on this planet, the value of human life is a product of supply and demand. It is precisely the fact that our days are numbered that makes each and every one of them incalculably precious to us. Our awareness of death is what makes us human. Any idea that dulls that awareness diminishes us in the long run, by undermining our fierce sense of urgency to make the most of each and every moment. Ingersoll agrees:

> *And so it may be, after all, that love is a little flower that grows on the crumbling edge of the grave. So it may be, that were it not for death there would be no love, and without love all life would be a curse.*

I think we need to stop seeing death as the negation of life, and see it instead as the necessary catalyst for every good thing we enjoy. This isn't just good sense, either; it's also good science. I'm no evolutionary biologist, but here's what I've learned from Ursula Goodenough's book, *The Sacred Depths of Nature:*

When a single-celled organism replicates, it gives birth to two new cells, but the parent cell never dies. In this way, you could say each of these organisms is actually immortal. As multi-celled animals emerge, however, they begin differentiating the cells involved in sexual reproduction (a.k.a. germ line) from those that handle the other jobs of being alive (a.k.a. somatic). In the process, somatic cell death is programmed in and immortality is handed over to the germ line. This liberates the soma—which for humans includes the brain—from any obligation to replicate, and allows it to focus instead on strategies for transmitting the germ line.

Whether or not you understand my little summary, you're sure to grasp Goodenough's conclusion:

So our brains, and hence our minds, are destined to die with the rest of the soma. And it is here that we arrive at one of the central ironies of human existence. Which is that our sentient brains are uniquely capable of experiencing deep regret and sorrow and fear at the prospect of our own death, yet it was the invention of death, the invention of the germ/soma dichotomy, that made possible the existence of our brains.

In other words, death is the price of awareness. Death is the price of love, joy, beauty, hope, and wonder. You can have immortality or you can have humanity, but you can't have both together. I don't know about you, but I choose this life. Or rather, I choose to be grateful for it, especially when I consider the infinitesimally small percentage of matter and energy in the universe that ever manages to animate at all, let alone as self-conscious human beings. Among secular thinkers, I think Richard Dawkins expresses this point best, in *Unweaving the Rainbow: Science, Delusion and the Appetite for Wonder* (1998):

> *We are going to die, and that makes us the lucky ones. Most people are never going to die because they are never going to be born. The potential people who could have been here in my place but who will in fact never see the light of day outnumber the sand grains of Arabia. Certainly those unborn ghosts include greater poets than Keats, scientists greater than Newton. We know this because the set of possible people allowed by our DNA so massively exceeds the set of actual people. In the teeth of these stupefying odds it is you and I, in our ordinariness, that are here. We privileged few, who won the lottery of birth against all odds, how dare we whine at our inevitable return to that prior state from which the vast majority have never stirred?*

To tell the truth, I am not afraid of returning to what Dawkins calls "that prior state." After all, once I've died there will be no "me" to be bothered by it. I agree with Epicurus: "Where death is, I am not, and where I am, death is not." Perhaps I might worry more about not existing if I didn't have so much experience, but I didn't exist for at least thirteen billion years before I was born, and it didn't trouble me at all. In reality, I consider this conscious life to be a brief, very exciting vacation from oblivion.

A few years ago my family and I were offered two weeks in the Hilton Head mansion of a generous friend, who threw in the keys to his speedboat and Jaguar convertible for good measure. Early on we were in heaven, lounging by the pool and enjoying vintage selections from our host's wine cellar, but as our departure date approached, I began lamenting the fact that we couldn't enjoy such luxury forever. It didn't seem fair that some families got to live that way all the time, but not mine. As Dawkins might put it, I began to whine.

It was my daughter, Miranda, who snapped me out of my funk, by reminding me how incredibly fortunate we were to be there in the first place, alive and healthy, basking in the sunshine together. "Look, Dad," she scolded me. "You can waste your last few days here moping around and wishing we could stay longer, or you can join the rest of us in squeezing out every last bit of happiness until it's time to go. Don't blow it. We both know that gratitude is the wiser choice."

Miranda was right, of course, and not just about those few days in South Carolina. Gratitude is always the wiser choice. Savor the food. Taste the wine. Enjoy the beach. And then, on the last day, if you're really smart, clean up the house, change all the sheets, and leave a nice note for the next people, wishing them as good a time as you've just had. Trust me, that's part of the fun too.

If you've ever been to a fabulous movie or ridden a thrilling roller coaster, you know what I'm talking about. In the buzz of excitement on the way out, as you pass the folks waiting in line for the next show, you can't help but nod and smile. "Ooh . . . you'd better buckle your seat belts!" you happily tell them. "You're really in for a wild ride!" Knowing the fun in store for someone else is a pleasure all its own.

I think one of the main reasons most people can't face death is that we haven't been very well trained to vicariously enjoy one another's happiness. We do a great job of teaching our kids to compete with each other, and sometimes we do equally well with cooperation, but when it comes to teaching them to openly delight in the accomplishments and good fortune of others—we haven't much practice. Too often we are too concerned with ourselves. And yet if there's one thing I'm sure of, it is this: Identifying with other people and using your imagination to vicariously enjoy their past, present, and future happiness is the key to dying well.

Here's a small example: While I'm still in relatively good health overall, both my ankles have been ruined by basketball injuries, bone spurs, lost cartilage, and arthritis. The bad news is that I'll never run or jump again, and practically every step I take is a painful adventure. The good news is that thanks to four operations and lots of ibuprofen, I can still walk reasonably well, not to mention ride my bike. The big question is what comes next.

Some people like me get bitter, lamenting the abilities they've lost and resenting anyone who still has them. They compare and complain, always looking backward and talking about how much they hate getting old. They become harder to bear, and as a result they feel more alone. Others, however, learn to let go more gracefully, in a way that actually accentuates their gratitude for what they had in the first place. "Wow," they say, "I can't run and jump anymore, but I sure did enjoy running and jumping when I could! Now I love to watch the young ones play, both to remember my own happiness and to celebrate theirs. When I can, I encourage them to truly revel in their youth, even as I remind myself to keep reveling in what's left of mine."

At the end of their lives, the happiest older men and women I know are invariably those who take the latter path. These elders know how to stand on the sidelines, offering wisdom and encouragement, while reminding themselves, "I don't need to be on the playing field anymore, in the center of the action. I had my time. It's their turn now." So then, I am working to become more of a cheerleader myself, so that at the end of my life, when I can't play at all, I am ready for it. "Working" is the key word in that last sentence, of course. Nobody has ever grown old and died gracefully by accident, and I know better than to think I'll be the first. This human dignity stuff requires sustained, conscious effort.

Of course, many of us haven't been very well trained to grieve, either, partly because so much of the time we are more concerned with convincing one another that our loved ones aren't really dead at all, but rather alive and well in a better place. Again, the fantasy of heaven often keeps us from focusing on what matters most.

A few years ago my family and I attended the funeral of Fritz Walker, who was the father of one of my closest friends and a big part of my life when I was growing up. For nearly three hours, friends and family members took turns sharing all kinds of touching stories that together vividly illustrated Fritz's unique brand of goodness. Finally, the minister in charge decided to wrap things up. Afterward, Fritz's son told me he and his siblings would have been happy to sit there all day. "Half of those stories we'd never heard before," he told me, "and even the ones we knew reached us in a different way. Learning other ways he'd touched people, other things he'd done, was like getting more of him, even though he's gone."

A good funeral laments the sadness of death, to be sure,

but it also celebrates the incredibly improbable privilege of life, and especially what my own father calls "those eternalized moments" when each of us is most fully alive. At a good funeral we are reminded that life is too precious to waste on trivial pursuits, and are inspired to renew our efforts to make the most of it by truly and deeply loving one another. The message shouldn't be "Joe isn't really gone," but rather "Wasn't he special? Aren't we lucky we got to know him? Isn't it amazing that any of us get to live at all?"

Of course, all of that is easier to do when we're talking about someone who lived a long and happy life. As a university chaplain, however, I often must face friends and family members who are reeling from the untimely death of a young person who will never get the chance to fulfill his or her human potential. It was the same when I served as a neighborhood minister in the inner city, except that often those young people were victims of violence as well. In any case, I think offering comfort after the death of a child is the ultimate test for any religious leader.

Some people think the theists get off easy by offering eternal life, but in my experience it is awfully difficult to reconcile the death of a child with the idea of a loving God. As a Christian, I knew what to say, but I don't think my words made much of a difference. What mattered most was just being there and sharing the hurt.

As a secular humanist, I mainly offer perspective. A few years ago one of my secular students lost his best friend in a car accident and came to me in great confusion.

"Look," I told him, "this is a terrible tragedy. Your friend Ben didn't get to experience seventy or eighty years, and that's not good and that's not fair. But still, he got to live! Ben wasn't a rock on Jupiter or a protozoa or even a spider. Ben was a person, and you loved him! And he felt your love. And he loved you back! It's not enough, of course, and even if it was, we'd always want more. But really, wasn't Tennyson right? Isn't it better to have loved and lost than never to have loved at all? Isn't it better that Ben lived and died than if he'd never lived at all? If that's true after a hundred years, then it's just as true after eighteen, or even after just a single minute of life. Stop and think for a moment: Babies can't understand or express it, but we know for a fact that they're capable of feeling. We also know that at the end of life, people often scratch and claw for just one more moment of that same awareness and sensation, even when it hurts. That's how precious each of those moments are, and your friend had some. This is the hard part, but however much or little we may get of it, this life is still the greatest bargain in the universe."

Of course, just as no amount of supernaturalism can wish away the pain of human suffering, no amount of secular perspective can actually make sense of a tragedy. The world we live in is amazingly beautiful, but it is also profoundly cruel and unjust. Indeed, though it produces animals like us, who care very much, the universe itself does not care at all. If there is to be any love or justice in this world, it falls to us to make it happen, and tragedies are our greatest reminders that we ought to get busy.

Really, for those of us who don't believe in personal immortality, the ultimate sin is to waste our precious time. That's what really frightens me, and my fear only grows as my perspective widens. The more I reflect on the infinite wonders of the universe, the sorrier I am that I have just one point of view, and a brief one at that. Try as I might to make the most of every opportunity, I sense that when the end comes I will want to cry out, "Oh no! Not yet! There's so much more I want to learn! There's so much more I want to see and do!"

Still, if I am honest, I don't want to live forever. I mean, even if you gave me a flawless body that would never decay, I'm pretty sure an unlimited experience of utopia would utterly overwhelm my demonstrably limited human mind. I suppose God could give me a boundless mind to match, but then I totally wouldn't be me, so really, what's the point? My finitude is a big part of my identity.

No matter how delicious a meal might be, at some point you're full. No matter how good a book or movie, at some point you want it to be over. No matter how delightful the party, at some point you're just too tired to enjoy it. You don't want to sing another song or hear another joke. You don't want to make any more friends. You've had enough. You're ready to go to sleep.

I'm a long way from that point, I think, but not so far that I can't already picture myself having had enough of this life and being ready to make room for someone else to take their turn. I can't imagine exhausting all the possibilities, mind you, but I can imagine being exhausted myself. Better still, I can imagine being satisfied.

I am not suggesting that the reality of death isn't painful, but just because something is painful doesn't mean it can be avoided, or even that it should be. I believe the promise of eternal life is a coping mechanism, and I don't like it. Pascal's famous wager posits that if there is even one chance in a million that God exists, you should bet your life on it, but to me those are terrible odds. Indeed, it may well be that the greatest mistake in this world is to live as if you have endless time when in fact you don't.

Not from Nowhere:
Why Transcendent
Experiences Point to God

by Tony Campolo

I OFTEN WISH THAT EVERYONE could spend a few hours a week in a really good Pentecostal worship service. In such churches, the power and presence of the Holy Spirit seem more tangible, which is very important. Being a Christian is much more than affirming doctrine, after all, as important as that may be. True discipleship is ultimately about having a personal encounter with the living Jesus, and *mystically* sensing His presence.

By the way, I believe that Jesus and the Holy Spirit are one and the same, and both are expressions of God the Father. As paradoxical as that may seem, like many Christians, I have actually experienced the truth of the doctrine of the Trinity. I grew up using the word "Father" for God, and that way of addressing God sometimes slips into my writings, but in reality the God I believe in transcends masculinity and femininity. To have a relationship with one member of the Trinity is to connect with all three. But then, that's another mystery, and most secularists do not leave much room for mysteries that transcend the empirical world of time and space. In contrast, I believe what is written in 1 Corinthians 2:9: *"Eye hath not seen, nor ear heard, neither have entered into the heart of man, the things which God hath prepared for them that love him"* (KJV).

Bart claims to be an up-to-date thinker, but I often think he is stuck in the thinking of a bygone century. It is especially interesting to me that he is so enamored of Robert Ingersoll, the popular late nineteenth-century atheist speaker and writer, who denied the existence of God in very dramatic ways. For example, while on the speaking circuit, Ingersoll would shock his audiences by holding up his pocket watch and declaring, "If there is a God, I challenge Him to strike me dead in the next sixty seconds." Then people would wait breathlessly in stunned silence as the next sixty seconds passed, after which the scoffers especially would break into applause.

What I believe Bart does not properly consider is that the kind of modern thinking championed by Ingersoll is increasingly outdated in this postmodern stage of history. In this new era, reducing reality to what can be understood only by empirical science has become passé, and there is an emerging consensus that there are forces at work in the universe that cannot be explored with empirical methods. Shakespeare's words in *Hamlet* ring truer today than when he wrote: "There are more things in heaven and earth, Horatio, than are dreamt of in your philosophy."

It disappoints me that so many secularists do not recognize inklings of the supernatural in the midst of our mundane world. They talk about affirming the awesomeness of the universe, but they can't really explain what generates this sense of wonder. Is it only the vastness of the universe that impresses them? Furthermore, those without faith persistently refuse to take seriously the many personal experiences reported by various people around the world, wherein spiritual forces unexpectedly break into their lives from beyond this empirical reality, creating overpowering effects. Such transcendent experiences shatter socially conditioned perceptions of the world, radiating an energy that can reasonably be regarded as supernatural. Rudolf Otto, the twentieth-century German scholar of comparative religions, called such nonrational experiences the *mysterium tremendum,* and I agree with him that they simply cannot be reduced to neurological functions of the brain.

Several years ago, after delivering a university lecture, I was challenged by a student who wanted to know how a sociologist with a Ph.D. could go on believing in God and trusting the Bible. This young man stood up and asked me why, given all the new psychological and neuroscientific information about human religiosity, I couldn't let go of what he referred to as "that old-time religion."

I was silent for a while, until the truest answer to that question became clear to me. "I believe in God because I decided to," I told him. "Then, having made that decision, I set about constructing theories and arguments to substantiate what I already had decided to believe."

"I thought so!" the young man said with a satisfied smile, shaking his head as he started to retake his seat.

"Wait!" I said. "Before you sit down, let me ask you why you don't believe in God, and why you *don't* trust that the Bible is inspired by God? Isn't it true that somewhere, at some point in your development, you decided *not* to believe in God, and *not* to accept the Bible as a possible revelation of truth from God? Since making those decisions, haven't you been constructing theories and arguments to support your *un*belief?"

My point was and is quite simple: On some level, faith is a choice. Certainly, I recognize that there are many different psychological and neuroscientific explanations for what I apprehend as the supernatural reality of God, but secularists too often forget that there is also the very real possibility that the biblical explanation will prove true in the end. As an evangelist, I encourage people to give the Gospel a chance, knowing that if they make that decision, the Holy Spirit will bear witness with their spirits that God is quite real and that they are God's children.

Blaise Pascal, one of the world's foremost mathematicians and philosophers, in his book *Pensées,* described a mystical experience that lifted him out of the mundane into an experience that was expressed by what he called, "Fire! Fire! Joy! Joy! Unspeakable joy!" Likewise, John Wesley, the founder of modern revivalism, had a mystical experience with God during a prayer meeting held in a Moravian assembly hall on Aldersgate Street in London. In his journal he describes how in that meeting his heart was "strangely warmed" in a way that assured him of his salvation and motivated him to preach the Gospel practically nonstop until his death.

William James, the prominent Harvard psychologist of the late nineteenth and early twentieth centuries, published a compilation of reports of such mystical encounters from people around the world. In his book, entitled *The Varieties of Religious Experience* (1902), James describes what he calls conversion experiences in this way:

To be converted, to be regenerated, to receive grace, to experience religion, to gain an assurance, are so many phrases which denote the process, gradual or sudden, by which a self hitherto divided, and consciously wrong, inferior and unhappy, becomes unified and consciously right, superior and happy, in consequence of its firmer hold upon religious realities. This at least is what conversion signifies in general terms, whether or not we believe that a direct divine operation is needed to bring such a moral change about.

I readily acknowledge that you would have to believe in God in order to claim that such conversions actually involve the Holy Spirit breaking into the consciousnesses of hurting people in order to heal and transform them. Some neuroscientists would claim that these mystical experiences are theoretically reducible to electrical impulses that stimulate specific areas of the brain. While I am not denying that the brain is stimulated during mystical experiences, I would contend that it is impossible to conclude which is the cause and which is the effect.

I feel the same way about the wonders of the universe, which secularists contend are nothing more than natural phenomena. Indeed, they go so far as to describe the existence of human beings—with all our physiological and intellectual complexities—as the intrinsically meaningless result of a series of random accidents of nature. Nevertheless, they tell us that in all likelihood there are more intelligent creatures in other parts of the universe. With an infinite extension of time, space, matter, and energy, they contend, organisms as complex as human beings are nearly certain to have emerged elsewhere as well. As Émile Borel famously put it, given enough time, even a chimpanzee punching at random on a typewriter would almost surely type out all the plays of William Shakespeare.

When considering evolution, however, we should reflect on the fact that many scientists do not believe that natural selection is simply a process of random trial and error. These scientists claim that there is something *within* organisms that *drives* them to make the needed adaptations for survival. In other words, the evolutionary development of living organisms is being guided. I am not a young earth creationist, but obviously I believe that the guiding force is the divine spirit we call God. So then, you can count me in with those oft-ridiculed religionists who claim there is an "intelligent designer" driving the creative processes of the universe.

Have I simply chosen to believe in a Creator who is revealed through the scriptures, who is at work in the conversions of broken people, and who regularly appears in my own life by way of transcendent spiritual experiences, and then cherry-picked those theories and arguments that best support that choice? Of course I have. Making that choice is my act of faith.

What I continue to wrestle with is why secularists like Bart choose to interpret the same raw data that I have in the opposite—and much less hopeful—direction. Surely to live as though there is nothing and no one behind the awesome wonder of the universe or our most transcendent experiences, and then cherry-pick the theories and arguments that best support that lifestyle, is an act of faith as well.

It's All in Your Head: How I Became a Religious Naturalist

by Bart Campolo

SOME OF MY SECULAR friends think I must be embarrassed about having said things like "I felt the presence of the Holy Spirit" and "God spoke to me" during my Christian days, but I'm not. On the contrary, I tell them, that stuff really happened. I actually sensed that there was someone else in the room, even though I was alone. I actually received messages about things I hadn't consciously considered all by myself. Those experiences were quite real to me, just as they continue to be quite real to millions of believers all over the world.

At that point, my secular friends often look at me as though I have betrayed both them and my own sense of reason, so I go on. If you don't believe in human experiences of transcendence, I say with a sly smile, then clearly you haven't attended the right rock concerts, or used the right drugs, or made love with the right partner, or been crowded into the right football stadium when the home team scores its winning touchdown on the last play of the game. Otherwise, you would know that we human beings aren't just *susceptible* to being overwhelmed by feelings of deep connection or oneness with other people, with nature, or with the universe itself; we are positively hardwired to crave and enjoy those feelings. Whether in the psychedelic euphoria of an LSD trip, the rhythmic energy of a tribal harvest celebration, or the august rapture of a cathedral choir swaying and singing hymns together by candlelight, people of all kinds actively seek out or proactively engineer those experiences that carry us beyond our everyday realities and connect us to ourselves and one another in positively transformative ways.

By the time I finish my discourse, my secular friends are generally smiling in recognition. Obviously, I explain, I interpret my earlier visitations from God differently now that I no longer believe in any kind of supernatural reality. These days I generally understand and explain them as psychological and neurological events that occurred in my brain. What I will never say, however, is that they didn't happen.

Dismissing the authenticity of spiritual experiences is a common mistake among secularists, I think, especially those who don't come from religious backgrounds. When people like that, who grew up with no firsthand exposure to the various ecstasies of supernatural faith, hear Christians making seemingly outlandish claims about their divine encounters, they often quickly conclude that such believers are lunatics, liars, or both. Not surprisingly, such dismissiveness is absolutely infuriating to any sincere believer, especially when it comes from a friend or family member, whether or not it is spoken aloud.

I know better than that, of course, because I've been on both sides of the fence. Actually, given my friendships with kind and devout Muslims, Jews, Hindus, Sikhs, Baha'is, and other kinds of believers, both before and after I left Christianity, I've been on both sides of more fences than I care to count. So then, while I am still no expert in interfaith dialogue, I am absolutely certain of this much: Genuine lunatics generally don't care whether you take them seriously, and almost nobody out there is lying about their transcendent experiences.

Even so, when someone tells me they've had a personal encounter with Jesus, I can't just accept that statement at face value. Again, while I absolutely believe that something real was happening in that moment, my best guess would be that they had an altogether natural personal experience of transcendence and, because they are Christian, interpreted that experience as a supernatural encounter with Jesus. I'm pretty sure that if that same person had that same transcendent experience as a Muslim, they would ascribe it to Allah instead, or if they were a Hindu, to Brahma, Shiva, or Vishnu. If, on the other hand, that person were a secular humanist like me, they would simply consider that experience to be one more natural wonder in this naturally wonderful universe, and thank their lucky stars that it happened.

In other words, as far as I can tell, all of us are prone to seek out or generate the same kinds of transcendent experiences. When they happen, however, each of us interprets them according to whatever worldview we hold at that moment, and uses them to confirm and validate that narrative. So then, one person's mysterious encounter with the living Jesus is another person's scientifically comprehensible neurological event, triggered and conditioned by a complex combination of psychological and environmental inputs.

In my case, the fact that transcendent experiences are entirely natural and in many ways increasingly understandable in scientific terms doesn't make them seem any less miraculously wonderful to me.

Everybody knows that today's roller coasters are exhaustively engineered to thrill and terrify their riders with seemingly death-defying drops, twists, and loops while being safer than a Sunday afternoon drive to the grocery store, but our awareness that our emotions are being expertly manipulated doesn't keep us from wanting to ride them. Movies work the same way. We know in advance that the filmmakers are going to make us laugh, cry, and sometimes scream in horror, but we still line up and pay for our tickets. Knowing how the process works doesn't destroy the experience; it actually enhances it, and we end up becoming especially loyal to those actors and directors who most reliably help us safely escape into realms of experience that would be otherwise impossible for us to reach.

As a gospel preacher I did the same thing from the pulpit, carefully calibrating my voice and body language as I told jokes and stories aimed at inspiring people to think about and feel my message in deep and transformative ways. It was my father who taught me how, of course, and while I have never been as good a communicator as he is, both of us know the power of a well-crafted, well-delivered sermon. Many preachers ascribe that power to the Holy Spirit, but that doesn't stop us from carefully taking into account what we wear, the layout and temperature of the room, what kind of music is played before and after we speak, and a hundred other environmental factors that can influence our audience's receptivity to what we have to say. On youth retreats, the most effective leaders extend that careful planning to include virtually every aspect of the experience, from who rides together in the vans and who bunks together in the cabins to what time people get to sleep and wake up, how the marshmallows get distributed at the campfire, and which kids get to share their testimonies. In a way, those leaders too are thrill-ride engineers, designing and manufacturing emotional roller coasters that bring young people to very specific decision points in just the right frame of mind.

Surprisingly, understanding those processes doesn't keep a great message or a well-executed retreat from having its desired impact. In fact, pulling back the curtain on emotional engineering generally relieves peoples' anxieties and suspicions that they might be taken advantage of, enabling them to get even more out of a transcendent experience. Learning how our brains and bodies work doesn't make them—or the experiences they make possible—any less amazing. On the contrary, it only adds more wonder.

Early in my secular journey, I noticed that biologist Ursula Goodenough describes herself as a religious naturalist. I love that moniker and only wish I could use it without being mistaken for some kind of Bible-toting trail hiker. Like Goodenough, I'm a naturalist because I think this physical universe—or multiverse, or whatever we're calling the totality of matter and energy these days—is all that is real. I'm religious not because I believe in a personal God or any other kind of supernatural force, but because I believe that natural reality—and in particular the parts of it that are alive and capable of transcendence—is more than wonderful enough to be worthy of my reverence, gratitude, and absolute devotion.

Don't get me wrong here—the fact that I pledge my allegiance to this world and this life doesn't mean that I think either of them has any overarching purpose or design. For better or worse, I'm afraid, my answer to that greatest of all philosophical questions—What is the meaning of life?—is that there isn't one. In short, the universe doesn't care.

We human beings do care, however, and that is my favorite part of the story of life. We still don't know how that story begins, of course, but thanks to Charles Darwin, we at least have a pretty good idea of how it moves forward from the simplicity of a single-celled something to the complexity of us, and somewhere along the way—right at the moment that animals started cooperating as a survival strategy—meaning emerged. That's because meaning isn't something we social animals *find,* after all, but rather something we *make* between us as we relate to one another.

That may well be the greatest wonder of them all, I think: That a cold and uncaring universe with no design or purpose whatsoever has nevertheless produced, at least on this one-in-a-billion planet in this one-in-a-billion galaxy, loving and lovable human beings like you and me, who desperately want to understand and appreciate ourselves and everything around us.

Obviously, I understand how and why my Christian friends believe there is someone actually driving the universe in a particular direction. I believed that myself for many years. Although I never bought into anything like traditional six-day creationism, it seemed to me there was no way all the complexity and interconnectedness within our bodies and our world were not the product of some sort of intelligent design, especially when I experienced those moments of transcendence that theologians like Paul Tillich and Pierre Teilhard de Chardin suggest are inklings of a spiritual reality that is essentially beyond human understanding. After all, how could something as intricate and delicately fine-tuned as our natural order happen by accident? Or, to be more precise, by an incredibly long series of incredibly improbable accidents?

The more I learn about the vastness of the universe, however, the less impossible that series of accidents seems to me. I'm not saying it isn't a kind of miracle, mind you, but only that amid all the trillions of stars and planets swirling through space over billions of years, such a miracle was bound to happen somewhere and at some point, and whatever self-conscious beings emerged out of it were bound to at least start out thinking it happened by design. In other words, until they found a way to look backward in time, whoever invented meaning was bound to think they'd received it instead.

I'm not sure we human beings are capable of fully describing the numinous qualities of life that give rise to so much religious conviction, let alone capable of fully controlling such blessings. I'm also not sure we'll ever be able to see backward in time far enough to fully understand where we come from or how we came to exist. Some people despair that science will someday remove all mystery from the universe, but I'm not worried. After all, as far as I can tell, every time we human beings answer a question or solve a problem, we simultaneously generate a dozen that are even more vexing. More important, even if we could explain it all, that wouldn't make this world any less precious or worthy of our devotion.

In the previous paragraph, I used the word "blessings" on purpose, because to me, any reality or human experience for which one can be thankful is a blessing. I no longer believe in a gracious God, but I still pause before every meal to give thanks for the food, for the hands that produced and prepared it, for the various parts of my body that enable me to enjoy it, and above all, for another day of conscious life, which is the greatest gift of all.

Who am I thanking, you may well ask? No one in particular, really, though perhaps I ought to at least consider my parents, my teachers, my friends, and all of our ancestors. Then again, given that every atom of every element on this planet—including those that form me—originated in the explosion of one or another conveniently located supernova millions of years ago, perhaps I should thank my lucky stars instead. In any case, I am deeply grateful for the many and various blessings of this life, and especially for those encounters with transcendence that I used to call divine appointments. Moreover, like my Christian friends, I find that openly expressing such gratitude heightens my awareness of those blessings in a way that makes them feel even more wonderful to me. Which is the point, after all.

A Joint Conclusion

by Bart and Tony Campolo

U<small>P TO THIS POINT</small>, it has been easy for our readers to know which one of us was doing the writing. The time has come, however, for both of us to write together in one voice. After all, we may disagree about the foundation of the universe and the ultimate destiny of humanity, but when it comes to navigating this life in between, we are and always have been of one mind: Love is the most excellent way.

The love we are talking about here, however, has less to do with flowery words and sweet emotions, and more to do with a fierce determination to know and be known by someone close and important to you, even when it is painful, so you can fully trust that person, even when you doubt his or her judgment.

That last part is especially relevant in our case, because clearly one of us is right about the essential truthfulness of Christianity, and the other one is wrong. The reality of God is not a matter of opinion, after all. One Campolo is thinking and moving in the right direction. The other one is terribly, perhaps even tragically mistaken. On this we are agreed.

Actually, after spending countless hours together—talking, listening, and becoming spiritually reacquainted—we stand in agreement on a great many things.

First and foremost, we agree that it is nearly impossible for people on opposite sides of the faith divide to have a warm, constructive conversation about religion and spirituality unless and until they first resolve to leave ultimate judgments about eternal salvation in the hands of God. Obviously, this does not present a problem for the secularist in the relationship, who by definition is already convinced that there are no eternal judgments to worry about. For the caring Christian, however, it is all too easy to become so frightened by the potential consequences of losing the argument that he or she becomes determined to win it by any means necessary, even if that means risking the relationship itself.

To Christians in danger of losing their tempers, becoming emotionally manipulative, or simply becoming paralyzed by fear, we offer this simple, biblical advice: Trust God. We're not just talking about obeying Jesus's commandment and promise, *"Judge not, and ye shall not be judged: condemn not, and ye shall not be condemned: forgive, and ye shall be forgiven"* (Luke 6:37, KJV), either, or taking seriously his illustration of the sheep and the goats in Matthew 25, whereby he makes clear that only God knows who will and won't enter into His Kingdom on Judgment Day. No, when we say "trust God," we mean that true believers should trust God's character, trust His infinite love for all of His children, and trust all those passages in scripture that suggest that God is able to do abundantly more than we could ever hope or pray or expect. None of us knows for sure what happens after we die, but the scriptures give Christians every reason to be optimistic and absolutely forbid any of us from speaking or acting as though we know God's specific plans for anyone else.

Consider a few examples:

The Lord is not slow about his promise, as some think of slowness, but is patient with you, not wanting any to perish, but all to come to repentance. (2 Peter 3:9, NRSV)

For surely I know the plans I have for you, says the Lord, plans for your welfare and not for harm, to give you a future with hope. (Jeremiah 29:11, NRSV)

For it is written,

> *"As I live, says the Lord, every knee shall bow to me,*
> *and every tongue shall give praise to God."* (Romans 14:11, NRSV)

[F]or as all die in Adam, so all will be made alive in Christ. (1 Corinthians 15:22, NRSV)

The saying is sure and worthy of full acceptance. For to this end we toil and struggle, because we have our hope set on the living God, who is the Savior of all people, especially of those who believe. (1 Timothy 4:9–10, NRSV)

Pray then in this way:

Our Father in heaven,
> *hallowed be your name.*
> *Your kingdom come.*

Your will be done,

    on earth as it is in heaven. (Matthew 6:9–10, NRSV)

Obviously there are plenty of other Bible verses that seem to contradict the idea that mercy triumphs over judgment, but in light of Jesus's example and overall message of grace and forgiveness, and his clear admonition against presuming to predict who will and won't be welcomed into heaven, we strongly suggest Christians trust that God's loving concern for their family members and friends far surpasses their own, and further trust that God will indeed have His way in the end.

This is not just good theology; it is also a good strategy for keeping the conversation going and maintaining close relationships across the faith divide. Simply stated, even when we know better, most of us feel deeply hurt and offended when we realize the person we are talking to genuinely believes we are doomed to hell. In a real sense, to write someone off that way is the ultimate act of disrespect, effectively negating every good thing they have ever said or done unless they change their mind and agree with us. Unfortunately, it is hard to meaningfully engage with someone who thinks of you as a "dead man walking."

We are not suggesting that is it easy for any evangelical Christian, and for parents especially, to stop worrying about the salvation of their nonbelieving loved ones and simply trust God with their ultimate welfare. Even now, despite a confidence in God's boundless grace that comforts him by day, Tony is still often troubled in the night by echoes of the hellfire-and-brimstone preaching he heard as a child, and the dire warnings of certain Bible verses. Nevertheless, when confronted by well-meaning "friends" who question Bart's eternal destiny, he has learned to respond in the simplest and most honest way: "Thanks for your concern, but I'm leaving that in the sure hands of God."

Something else the two of us agree on is the need for both parties in this conversation to be more interested in listening to and understanding the other person than in convincing them to change their mind. Over and over again we have talked to other fathers and sons and mothers and daughters whose greatest sadness is not that their loved one doesn't agree with them, but rather that they don't seem interested at all in understanding what they've experienced, why they think or believe the things they do, or how they feel about their spiritual journey. Again, sometimes this seeming lack of interest is purely a function of fear, but other times it has more to do with the familiar patterns that often grow up in a family. It is no accident that the conversations that laid the groundwork for this book happened when we stepped out of our usual patterns of relating, set aside special times and places to talk, and both resolved in advance to start out by listening without interruption, and asking questions only for the sake of clarity, and not as a form of attack.

Don't get us wrong—we broke those resolutions many times, and often had to apologize to each other for interruptions, harsh words, sarcastic or condescending comments, and just plain not listening. Truly, it is a good thing that both of our religions place a premium on humility and forgiveness, because unless we had loads of practice at both offering and accepting apologies, we never could have made it this far together. Sometimes, when face-to-face talking failed us, we resorted to long e-mails, or pointed each other to books or articles that expressed our thoughts better than we could ourselves. It was harder in the beginning, when each of us thought the other might actually come around, but it became a lot more fun later on, once both of us realized our fundamental values and most urgent ministry concerns weren't nearly as different as they first seemed.

Years ago, when Tony was Bart's current age and Bart was a newly married urban missionary, we wrote another book called *Things We Wish We Had Said,* which was essentially all about raising thoughtful, compassionate, justice-oriented Christians. Reading it over now, both of us are wistful about our almost casual like-mindedness when it came to theology, but also surprised by how much has remained constant within and between us, despite all the obvious changes. Then as now, we both were convinced that people—and young people especially—are hardwired for heroism and can feel truly happy and fulfilled only when called upon to sacrificially use their gifts and energies in the service of a noble cause much bigger than themselves. Now as then, we both are obsessed with finding more and better ways to call them to such causes.

In the end, however, all the new technologies in the world haven't yet challenged or changed the most essential fact of missionary recruiting: What moves people most are stories. Jesus knew that, of course, and so did the Gospel writers who told His story. Then again, the Old Testament is full of stories too, and so is the Koran, the Bhagavad Gita, and virtually every other holy book on the planet. Charles Darwin told a somewhat different story from those about where we come from, and Albert Einstein told still another later on, which started much farther back in time. Which of all those stories is true or most true is beside the point here; what matters is the simple fact that we human beings have always needed and used stories to make sense of the world and find our place in it. If you want to touch somebody's heart and mind in a way that actually changes their life, you have to tell stories.

Both of us have spent most of our adult lives telling stories about the needs of people around the world who are hurt, oppressed, neglected, impoverished, or otherwise left out of those blessings the rest of us enjoy. We also tell stories about ordinary people who have responded to those needs in extraordinarily loving ways, always trying to illustrate the lesson we have learned from them over and over again: Caring for others is the surest pathway to peace. As Bart's agnostic hero Robert Ingersoll once put it, "The way to be happy is to make others so." Or, in the words of St. Francis, "For it is in giving that we receive."

In our storytelling, we do our best to highlight the value of thoughtful sacrifice and the beauty of practical love. We talk about the good works of inner-city schoolteachers, rural doctors and nurses, crusading lawyers, compassionate neighbors, adoptive parents, nurturing camp counselors, AA sponsors, socially responsible businesspeople, climate change activists, LGBTQ allies, and various Good Samaritans, all of whom demonstrate the transformative power that lies within every one of us, waiting to be released in the service of others. We don't pretend we're not appealing to our audiences' emotions, either; really, that's the main point of most of our stories. After all, when you are a gospel preacher, you're always aiming for the heart.

Obviously, each of us grounds his "here and now" call to sacrificial service in a very different grand narrative about the nature and destiny of the universe, and that is no small matter. There is a big difference between wisely investing the earthly portion of your life to help build the eternal Kingdom of God and wisely spending your precious few years of consciousness expressing your gratitude by paying it forward. If you've heard us preach, then you know that difference generally shows up at the end. Tony finishes his sermons by proclaiming that no matter how bad things may be ("It's Friday . . ."), Almighty God will surely prevail in the end (". . . but Sunday's comin'!"). Bart wraps up his by asserting that humanity's uncertain future ("The universe is random and without purpose . . .") only enhances our gloriously improbable opportunity in the meantime (". . . but we can manufacture meaning in our relationships"). What both of us instinctively grasp, however, is that it is only when we connect our own little stories to that overarching grand narrative which we most truly believe that people like us are inspired to reach our full potential. And so we preach on.

At the end of the fourth century, writing to Christians willfully ignorant of Greek, mathematics, and music in favor of pure devotion to studying the Bible, St. Augustine said:

> We ought not to give up music because of the superstition of the heathen, if we can derive anything from it that is of use for the understanding of Holy Scripture; nor does it follow that we must . . . refuse to learn letters because they say that Mercury discovered them; nor because they have dedicated temples to Justice and Virtue, and prefer to worship in the form of stones things that ought to have their place in the heart, ought we on that account to forsake justice and virtue. Nay, but let every good and true Christian understand that wherever truth may be found, it belongs to his Master.

Later writers paraphrased this thought into the popular aphorism "All truth is God's truth" to remind themselves that God reveals Himself not only in scripture but also in nature, conscience, and history. This idea—which theologians refer to as general revelation—is very encouraging for Christians who enjoy and appreciate such disparate endeavors as science, fictional literature, and the dramatic arts, and even more so for those eager for interfaith engagement. In our case, it gives Tony every reason to respectfully pay attention to Bart's life and ministry, in case there is something good for him to learn.

Of course, as far as we are concerned, the reverse of that aphorism—which we clumsily offer as "Factual or not, Christianity and the world's other supernatural religions express some profound truths in rich and timeless ways"—is equally valid. Conveniently, this enables Bart not to despise all those years he spent following Jesus, and further gives him every reason to respectfully pay attention to Tony's life and ministry, in case there is something good for him to learn . . . or remember . . . or even borrow, with a few small tweaks. Like this passage from Isaiah 65 (NRSV), which beautifully envisions the world we both long for:

> For I am about to create new heavens
> and a new earth;
> the former things shall not be remembered
> or come to mind.
> But be glad and rejoice forever
> in what I am creating;
> for I am about to create Jerusalem as a joy,
> and its people as a delight.
> I will rejoice in Jerusalem,
> and delight in my people;
> no more shall the sound of weeping be heard in it,

or the cry of distress.

No more shall there be in it

an infant that lives but a few days,

or an old person who does not live out a lifetime;

for one who dies at a hundred years will be considered a youth,

and one who falls short of a hundred will be considered accursed.

They shall build houses and inhabit them;

they shall plant vineyards and eat their fruit.

They shall not build and another inhabit;

they shall not plant and another eat;

for like the days of a tree shall the days of my people be,

and my chosen shall long enjoy the work of their hands.

They shall not labour in vain,

or bear children for calamity;

for they shall be offspring blessed by the LORD—

and their descendants as well.

Before they call I will answer,

while they are yet speaking I will hear.

The wolf and the lamb shall feed together,

the lion shall eat straw like the ox;

but the serpent—it's food shall be dust!

They shall not hurt or destroy

on all my holy mountain,

says the LORD.

It may well be that one day, someday, Bart will see this heavenly vision realized and understand for all time that he was utterly mistaken about where it came from. Or perhaps, if Bart is right, Tony will close his eyes in the end and never discover that this mortal life was the only one he had in which to pursue it. In the end, undeniably, each of us believes the other is missing out on something infinitely valuable by persisting in his foolishness.

What neither of us believes, however, is that the other is a fool. As we said at the beginning, while we come to it differently, each of us always reaches the same conclusion about this life: Love is the most excellent way. Moreover, each of us is both sure and content that the other has found that way. For now, at least, that is enough.

Acknowledgments

Books are seldom produced easily, and never alone.

Both of us are immensely grateful to Marty Campolo, Sarah Blaisdell, Gavin Hewitt, John Wright, Robert Barr, and Mark Sweeney for the many and various ways they kindly helped us produce the original manuscript of the book, and to Lisa Zuniga for gently turning that manuscript into something publishable.

We are also grateful to Mickey Maudlin, for lending us his vast experience and insight, and for giving us the encouragement we needed at just the moments we needed it most. His wisdom and patience are legendary for good reason.

There are countless others, of course, to whom we owe more than we can ever repay for teaching, encouraging, and supporting us over the years. Some are named in these pages, but we trust the rest of you know who you are and how much we appreciate you.

Finally, we are grateful for Peggy Campolo, whose immense contributions, not only to this book but also to the lives behind it, truly cannot be overstated. Without her, there would be no us.